Walking Man

A Modern Missions Experience in Latin America

By Narciso Zamora

Afterword by Michael Cassidy
Founder, African Enterprise

The Quilldriver
WORKS WITH WORDS

Clarksville, Arkansas

Walking Man: A Modern Missions Experience in Latin America
By Narciso Zamora
Afterword by Michael Cassidy, Founder of African Enterprise

Translated by Donna L. Schillinger from original text,
Caminante con Dios by Narciso Zamora
Cover Photo by Matthew Fraser
Cover Design by Kevin Greenblat Creative
Map Illustration by Jordan Bass, Map Photo ©Jamie Cross-FOTALIA

A publication of
The Quilldriver
PO Box 573
Clarksville, AR 72830 U.S.A.
info@thequilldriver.com
www.thequilldriver.com

Edition ISBNs
Softcover English   978-0-9791639-0-6
Softcover Spanish *Caminante con Dios*   978-0-9791639-1-3
Audio, MP3 English   978-0-9791639-2-0
Audio, MP3 Spanish *Caminante con Dios*   978-0-9791639-3-7
PDF English   978-0-9791639-4-4

Publisher's Cataloging-In-Publication Data
(Prepared by The Donohue Group, Inc.)
Zamora, Narciso.
   [Caminante con Dios. English]
   Walking man : a modern missions experience in Latin America /
by Narciso Zamora ; afterword by Michael Cassidy ; translated by Donna L. Schillinger.
   p. : map ; cm.
   Translation of: Caminante con Dios.
   ISBN: 978-0-9791639-0-6
1. Zamora, Narciso. 2. Missionaries--Latin America--Biography. 3. Church of God
(Anderson, Ind.)--Missions--Latin America. I. Schillinger, Donna L. II. Title.
BV3705.Z36 A3 2007
266.9/092

Printed in the United States of America

Publisher/Translator's Note

When my grandmother, Evelyn Anderson of Christian Triumph Company, learned I was going to serve in the Peace Corps in Ecuador, she told me she had a friend there, Narciso Zamora. She wrote him to tell him I was going to be living in Ecuador for two years.

My first stop in the Peace Corps was a training center in Tumbaco, Ecuador, a 30-minute bus ride from Quito, about an hour from the area of Quito where Narciso and his family were building their home and church, a neighborhood called Comité del Pueblo.

One day, the training center staff called me out of class, saying I had a visitor. It was Narciso. Upon receiving my grandmother's letter, he had taken it on himself to make the two-hour round trip by bus and walk another two miles round trip to meet me. He acted like it was an honor to meet me and invited me to his church. I didn't understand. Did he want something from me?

Though perplexed, I eventually attended his church, and when I was assigned to my permanent post in Quito, I became well acquainted with and quite fond of the Zamora family, and I attended church occasionally. I also participated in some of the events Narciso writes of, such as the church-building work camps.

Some months after my return to the United States, I received a package in the mail from Narciso, it was the manuscript of this book in Spanish, originally titled, "The Missionary Work in Latin America." Narciso asked me to translate it. I kept it in a drawer with the good intention of getting around to it until one day, my grandmother asked for the manuscript back. I had never even read it.

More than a decade later, I got in the mail a copy of the book published in Spanish, autographed by the author. I realized this was the book I had never translated. Out of curiosity, I started to read. I took it to court with me as I awaited cases to interpret for Spanish defendants or witnesses. It helped keep me "in Spanish mode."

Though I had many dealings with Narciso and his family since my days in Quito, including hosting him in my home and being a guest in his home in Chile, I never really had figured out that Walking Man who had made an awfully long trip to meet me, a total stranger, until I read the book. Only then did I understand that the effort he had put forth to meet me was like a walk in the park compared to the strides and lengths he'd taken to reach out to even a few total strangers in remote jungle and mountain regions.

Before I even finished reading the book in Spanish, I felt God saying to me, "I'm giving you another chance to translate this. Do it now." So I began to translate the work and determined to publish it, as well.

Is *Walking Man* special to me? You had better believe it. Not only do I count the author among one of my oldest friends, this book has been my impetus to make a career shift of which I'd dreamed.

In my first pass, I translated the book as close to word-for-word as I could. Then as an editor personally acquainted with the author, I worked with the translation to give it the English equivalent sound of the Narciso I know – the zealous, completely dedicated and humble man of God I feel honored to help English speakers come to know better.

Thanks to some essential feedback from early manuscript reviewers, Juli Ginn, Nancy Hunter and Amy Torres, I have come to understand that though there are universal elements to this story, particularly those pertaining to our walk with God, there are also elements in Narciso's story that are clearly of another culture and may seem unusual (at best) to American readers. The division of labor in Latin America, for instance, is still quite distinct between men and women – more like America of the 1950s. When we read of Narciso's wife, Udelia Zamora's role in her marriage and the Zamora ministry, we must put it in the perspective of the more male-dominant Latin culture. And what about the very thing that always struck me as strange about Narciso – the great effort to which he goes to do something simple – days and days of journey just to take the Good News to a few people? For many Americans, the ratio of effort to benefit seems out of whack. For Narciso, effort seems not to be even in the equation.

As a typical American traveler, I also marvel at how Narciso would start out on long journeys without so much as a lunch box, not to mention a few layers of clothing to add when he climbed to the alpine zone. It is much more common in Latin America and other parts of the world for the traveler to expect a certain trust, hospitality and generosity to be extended to him to provide for his needs and keep his burden light along the way.

Another way in which this manuscript is "foreign" is that it lacks the structure American readers often expect in a plot. Instead of foreshadowing building to a climactic point with a resolution to cap it all off nicely, this literary journey is more like a walk through the Andes Mountains – it has ups and downs and more ups and more downs, sometimes prompting us to wonder where we're headed. In fact, this story is just the chronicle of a journey of a thousand miles, both literal and figurative. We've pointed out some vista points for reflexion along the way with discussion primers.

Lastly, in case this narrative leaves you wondering about what happens between the time Narciso introduces a character to his narrative and that same person accepts Christ only a sentence or two later, we've included an afterword by seasoned evangelist and founder of African Enterprise, Michael Cassidy. Michael so beautifully details the necessary dialogue to lead a person to Christ that you may want to keep this book in your glove box in case God calls you to action.

We hope that when you've finished this leg of the journey, you'll be inspired to walk further, be it in your own direction with other missions you know of and can participate in and contribute to, or walk on with Narciso at www.walkingman.ws, where you'll find pictures from his ministry and more about his sons' ministries and learn how you can partner with the Walking Man in his efforts to train Latin American men and women to fulfill the Great Commission in their own countries and continent.

Just your purchase of this book has helped. A significant portion of both author's and publisher's proceeds are going directly back into this ministry in Latin America. If this book inspires you, please consider passing it on to a friend or purchasing a copy for your church library. See our convenient order form on the last page and our "no shipping and no sales tax" special offer.

In addition to the reviewers I mentioned earlier, I would also like to thank my good friend Jamie Morrison, formerly of African Enterprise, for helping raise this book to a higher level. And of course, my husband, John, and daughter, Gwen, for their indulgence.

Donna Schillinger

Points of Interest in South America on the Walking Man's Journey

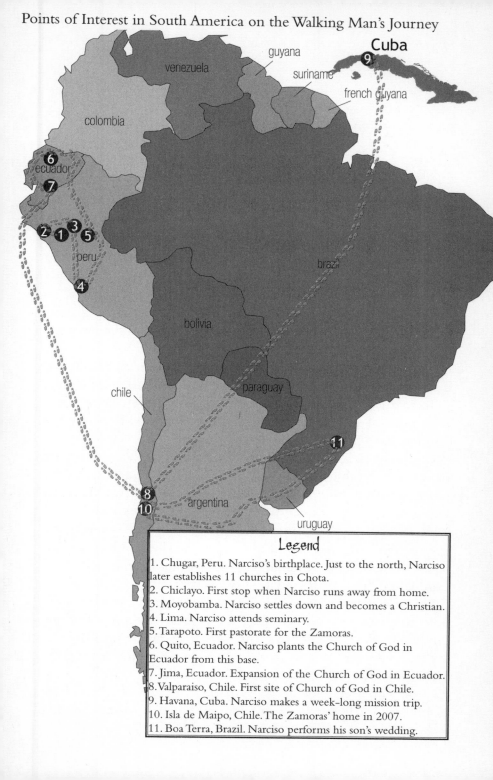

Legend

1. Chugar, Peru. Narciso's birthplace. Just to the north, Narciso later establishes 11 churches in Chota.
2. Chiclayo. First stop when Narciso runs away from home.
3. Moyobamba. Narciso settles down and becomes a Christian.
4. Lima. Narciso attends seminary.
5. Tarapoto. First pastorate for the Zamoras.
6. Quito, Ecuador. Narciso plants the Church of God in Ecuador from this base.
7. Jima, Ecuador. Expansion of the Church of God in Ecuador.
8. Valparaiso, Chile. First site of Church of God in Chile.
9. Havana, Cuba. Narciso makes a week-long mission trip.
10. Isla de Maipo, Chile. The Zamoras' home in 2007.
11. Boa Terra, Brazil. Narciso performs his son's wedding.

Prologue

There are unforgettable lives like those of the Apostle Peter, Paul, Martin Luther and others. Mine is certainly not of that stature, but this autobiography does attempt to inspire triumph in the midst of adversity – be it illness, insult, slander, betrayal or great adventure. I feel blessed to have lived and prevailed through all of these.

Although I hope you'll find my story engaging to the last page, my prayer is that my testimony will glorify Christ.

When I first believed in Jesus and even later when I enrolled in the Theology Bible Institute, I had not considered nor even wished to be in missions. I was studying with the idea of returning to the place where I was saved; with all my heart I wanted to help those brothers since they had helped me so much.

I got into missions inadvertently. I had to sell clothing to support my family, traveling each week to different communities in the provinces of San Martin de la Selva and Cajamarca, Peru. My transportation included trucks, small aircraft, boats, horses and, more often than not, my own two feet. When I got where I was going, people were saved because, in addition to the clothes I had brought to sell, I also brought with me tracts to minister in the work of our Lord Jesus Christ. God used me marvelously.

I never made much money selling clothes after all, but many souls accepted Jesus and were saved by the grace of God. My clothing business opened the door to the mission field, the business of Jesus. It's by far the best and we're still in his business today, serving the Lord with great joy.

To all who want to be ministers of the word and are called by the Lord: Pray, study the word and commit yourself to entering the battle. You can't expect a crown if you don't enter the race. Jesus is King. You have to prepare yourself to laugh and to cry, too – but the will of God is that we live a joyful life.

I want to thank my wife Udelia and my sons, Gerson and Eliezer, for their great dedication to the service of the Lord and to the church, and for the help and support they have given me.

"We are hard pressed on every side, but not crushed; perplexed, but not in despair; persecuted, but not abandoned; struck down, but not destroyed. We always carry around in our body the death of Jesus, so that the life of Jesus may also be revealed in our body." II Corinthians 4:8-10 (NIV).

The Cross of My Childhood

Mountains lush with trees through which the sun breaks at dawn surround a green field. Swallows and other birds trill and the pigeons fly in flocks around a small cabin with a thatched hay roof and walls of thin, round eucalyptus. Oak posts are spaced so that rays of sun pass through, as does the cold.

It was in such a nook that I was born in the month of May in the 1950s in a little place called Tacamache, in the district of Chugur, province of Hualgayoc, state of Cajamarca in Peru. My parents, Marcial Zamora and Gricelida Fernández, were very nervous in my first days on earth because only days after I was born, I became very ill. Obviously, I won that battle and infirmity and death did not accomplish their objectives. Thanks to the natural herbs of the country that God provided, my condition stabilized and my body was healed. With God's help, I was victorious for the first time over illness.

My parents were a couple of young, poor country kids, with little formal learning or culture. They had very little money, clothing or furniture in the house. My mother had suffered for several years with a chronic illness. My father worried and seemed always to be searching for some medicine to cure her. He resorted to witchdoctors, healers, charmers, doctors, surgeons and naturalists. They finally took her to the Medical Center of Bambamarca, an almost 12-hour horseback ride. The doctors didn't hold out any hope of her survival.

When they arrived home again, we all thought she would die soon. In desperation, my father visited the Roman Catholic Church to pray. As he entered, he rushed toward a statue and fell to his knees to plead for my mother's recovery.

During this time, for several years in a row, my parents visited the Virgin of Remedies in a place called Liscan. My older sister,

Gumercinda, my brother Rocel and I would stay at home for an entire week while my parents were gone to ask the Virgin to cure my mother.

They began to lose hope as Mother's health remained unchanged. As a last resort, we gathered herbs from the countryside. My sister ground them on a very large rock and mixed them with boiled water and coarse brown sugar. We gave this to my mother every morning and afternoon. After being on this regimen for a while, thank God, she began to improve and continued to take the herbs until she was cured.

〰

When I was seven years old I started elementary school – it was the 1960s. We didn't wear uniforms because it was a country school and the children were too poor. Despite our daily hardships, I always tried to arrive early to my classes. My brother Rocel and I took off running every morning from our house toward the school. It was a 20-minute barefoot walk. In the afternoon, when school let out, I liked to play soccer.

Later, we worked in the fields with my father. On Sundays, my father would sell potatoes, beans, dried peas and other produce in the city. He would mount up 80 kilos of produce on his mule and travel to the city of Lajas or Yauyucan. With the money he made he bought kerosene, detergent, salt, matches and some cookies. He would always arrive home drunk.

When he went out to a party or festival, he might stay out all night. Often he took my mother with him and, faithful companion that she was, she never left him passed out in the road. She was always at his side.

Sometimes my father would get drunk when we went out as a family, and then about midnight we would head out toward home. It didn't matter if we were a two-hour walk from home, we had to walk in the pitch black on rocky roads that were also often muddy. My recollection of those nights was of being scared to death, cold and crying as I walked behind my drunken father – who wasn't feeling a thing.

$$\approx$$

Peru is as relatively undeveloped today as it was in my youth. However, even by standards of an underdeveloped country my family was poor. We had no luxuries and lacked even some of the basics of an average Peruvian household of the time. For instance, I never tasted white sugar or coffee until I was about 12 years old. We never had white sugar at home because it was so expensive. And instead of the morning coffee that is a custom in Spanish-speaking countries, my parents would give us warm soup (which may be more nutritious but was an indicator of our poverty).

We wore plain cotton pants and tank tops and ran around without shoes. In winter months, there was frost on the ground and our feet would crack open and bleed. What an excruciating pain – sometimes I just couldn't take it. When we had to travel to Perlamayo to work, we walked in the frosted fields. When the farmers would make a cow get up to go and be milked, Rocel and I would run over to stand in the spot where the cow had been lying because that spot would be warm. I never knew what a jacket or a sweater was but my mother made wool ponchos for us to use against the cold. Our toys were corn cobs, though we hardly ever had time to play with them because we always seemed to be working in the fields or taking care of our sheep.

When school was out for vacation, we spent our time farming vegetables – greens, potatoes, corn. (All this we had planted for our own food. We sold only a little of it.) While still a child, I learned to use a hoe, spade and machete. We didn't do much else on vacation – just three months of work, work, work.

I always used to wonder why there are so many people who suffered. I wondered why people had to spend their whole lives working and still they didn't have enough to eat at times. And then they died.

The better part of my life's story has poverty as a theme. Since knowing Jesus, I have taken hope in his words recorded in Luke

4:18, "The Spirit of the Lord is on me, because he has anointed me to preach good news to the poor." I believe it's the will of God that we serve him despite our poverty – and not let that be an obstacle for serving Jesus.

God's Care for Me

I thank God that long before I began to serve him, the Lord Jesus was taking care of me. When I was 13 years old, I had an accident. I fell from a horse onto some rocks. I broke my left ankle and my pelvic bone. After a few minutes I got up, and though I could hardly walk, I took the horse by its bridle and limped from Pampa Grande to Uncle Fortunato Zamora's house. I was dragging my injured foot and walking in the pouring rain besides. My father had taken some other horses loaded with hay to build our kitchen roof and I was left alone with no one to help me.

Taking it slowly and crying in pain all the way, I finally arrived at about 7:00 p.m. All night long I groaned from the pain in my foot which had swollen considerably. The next day my father put me on a mule and took me to a country bone fixer to have the bone set to heal. As I was getting down off the mule, I thought, Please let this not hurt!

A tall man with a dark red poncho had me sit down on a tree trunk; he took my foot and started sliding his hand over it. I started to scream. He softly placed the bone and then bandaged the ankle with a piece of cloth. Only one week later, my ankle was better – it had healed.

〰〰

When I finished junior high school, my parents decided that I should continue in school despite the precarious conditions in which we lived, that is, in poverty. We didn't have enough money to buy salt but they wanted me to continue my education. It was a very risky decision as they had seven more sons! My older sister was the only one who stayed at home after elementary school so that she could help my parents working in the home.

My first year of secondary school marked the first time in my life that I wore shoes – made of plastic. My parents sold their only cow to pay for my uniform, books and supplies.

In 1970 and 1971, I studied at El Señor de los Milagros (The Lord of Miracles) in Ninabamba, a school out in the country. My mother would wake up at 4:30 a.m. to prepare a hot vegetable broth for our breakfast and cook potatoes for me to take to school for lunch. Sometimes my sister Gumer woke up early to help Mother.

Rocel and I sat next to Mother as she served us the very hot soup. While we ate, Mother put the potatoes in a plate and covered them with another plate and wrapped them up in a white cloth. We put the lunch in our pack and we were ready to go.

We left for school at 6:30 a.m. because it took us one hour on foot to make the journey to school. There was a stream near the school where we would stop and wash our faces and feet, which were muddy by the time we arrived. Very near the school was a room for which we had paid a fee to use to keep our school uniforms. We would change into them just before we went to school.

The school had 500 students. At noon, we would get out of class to eat, and we didn't resume classes until 2:00 p.m., taking the long break for the customary siesta. At 5:00 p.m., we headed back home and would arrive at 6:30 or 7:00 p.m. My mother always had our dinner piping hot, ready and waiting in a big, three-legged clay pot that sat on top of an open fire. After we ate, we lit a kerosene lantern so we could do all our chores and homework. We stayed up studying until 11:00 each night.

For four years my mother sacrificed to get up early every morning to make our lunch.

My First Adventure

In 1973 when I was in my late teens, I ran away from home. It was the month of April, a rainy month. I was leaving home for the first time – without telling my parents – I just could not fathom a life of back-breaking labor and drunken weekends. After walking for about five hours and having climbed all the way up Mt. Coyunde, I stopped and looked at the house where I was born and I cried for a moment. I started walking again and by the afternoon, I arrived in Lajas where I waited for a bus that passed by at night from Chota on the way to Chiclayo. I didn't know how to get the bus to stop so I asked a young man if he would do it for me. I felt silly when I realized how simple it was — just raising my hand as the bus approached.

I got on the bus and took a window seat in the middle. At that moment my anguish began — the trip was making me ill — motion sick — and I arrived in Chiclayo quite sick. As we got off the bus, a man who had also been a passenger offered to pay for a hotel room for me, which was very generous of him considering that I was a stranger. I slept peacefully that night and the next day I went out looking for work.

I went to a bus station called Noreste and a tall, dark man came up and offered me work. It was a con, though. As we spoke, he was actually robbing me of what little money I had.

That night I slept in the doorway of the bus station.

The next day, I went walking down a particular street and a young man came up to me and said, "Do you want to work? We need boys to sell pastries."

I didn't know anything about that city and I didn't have any skills. I didn't even know how to use a broom — but that very day I started to work selling pastries. I made enough to eat and to get a place to sleep, thank God.

I sold pastries in the major market of Chiclayo, a city that was full of delinquents and thieves. I didn't do very well because I was always being robbed of my money or the pastries. It seemed all I ever met were juvenile delinquents, so I decided to leave that city and head for the Peruvian jungle.

I traveled for a day and a half in a truck and finally arrived in Bagua, and from there I went on to Chachapoyas with my bag in hand. I walked through the city of Chachapoyas and that afternoon I met a gentleman sitting on a park bench and he offered me work.

I was desperate. The words were hardly out of his mouth before

I was eagerly accepting. He invited me to travel with him and work in a community called Quispe. I said I would, so that night he took me to dine and spend the night with one of his relatives in Chachapoyas.

The next day we traveled six hours in a small bus to Luya, a very small, quaint town. We spent that night in the house of the postmaster, who was the niece of the man I was traveling with, and she made humitas (a sweet cornbread) for us and gave us a good bed to sleep in.

The next morning we headed out to Quispe. My boss, so to speak, rode a horse and I had to walk what was to be a 25-hour hike. I met a young man on the road and we started talking. I told him what I was doing and where I was going.

He stopped, looked at me and said, "You're crazy! How can you go to that place? It's very dangerous and very far away. You'll never come back!"

I thought for a moment and then slipped quietly into an irrigation ditch. The irrigation canal was under construction, so I hid there all day. My boss probably thought I had fallen a little behind since he was on horse and I was walking. He didn't come back looking for me.

When I got up out of the ditch, I started to run until I arrived back at Luya. From there I went to Lamud, a very small town about four kilometers away. There I quickly got another job selling pastries, this time at the entrance to a high school.

Each night I would help make the pastries and then sell them the next day. One night, I worked all night without stopping – making the jellies and mixing the pastry dough. I was so tired when the morning came but I still had to be at the high school at 9:00 a.m. to sell the pastries. That morning I fell asleep and stayed that way as the students came out for recess. They saw me sleeping and ate all the pastries. I had to go home with no pastries and no money. The boss made me work that off, which took two months.

One Monday afternoon, the boss left to go purchase fruit and supplies to make jelly and I knew he wouldn't be back for a while. I took advantage of that time to break into the room where he kept the money and I took enough money for a bus ticket and to hold me over for a few days. That same day I headed out on a bus to Chachapoyas.

I arrived there in the afternoon and just started walking the streets looking for a job. A man who was leaning up against a truck called me over and said, "Do you want to work?"

"Yes!" I answered.

He said he had a job for me, he took me home with him, gave me a cup of coffee and then showed me the work — it was making mattresses out of rice straw. I had to sleep in the straw.

Lacking enthusiasm for that task, as well, early the next morning I slowly opened the door and crept out into the street with my bag in hand. I caught a truck to a town called Pedro Ruiz Gallo which was about two hours away.

In that place, I met a woman who sold fruit in a kiosk. She gave me food and a place to stay for three days. Then a man who sold wood employed me for three weeks to go out into the orchards and fields and plant fruits and vegetables. In the afternoons, I could eat all the fruit I wanted.

After that job, I went back to Chiclayo, courtesy of two men who were hauling machines for the army and needed someone to show them the way to Chiclayo. I helped out the army in exchange for a hot lunch that day — I ate with the captain and other officers! That was a very delicious meal.

It took us two days to get to Chiclayo. Since I didn't have any money when I arrived, I joined up with three other young men who slept in a school. That didn't last long before I was off again — this time to the big city. I decided to go to Lima, the capital, to try my luck. And there I met some serious juvenile delinquents and became one of them. I lived by thievery.

One Wednesday morning, I happened to meet my uncle Aníbal in Union Square. He took me straight to the police for my mischief and then he took me home with him.

Near the end of 1975, I returned home for a while but I was still restless. My parents were glad to have me home but worried about me, naturally.

I asked my father for a ride one day to another town called Santa Cruz and on that trip he asked me, "Where are you going, son? I want to know."

I replied, "I really don't know where I'm going. I'm just wandering."

〰

I spent some time in a very picturesque town called Pomacochas, situated next to a lake with thatched-topped homes. The lake was stocked full of fish for the taking. There were many legends about that lake. People told stories of sirens that lived in an ancient, evil city that had been flooded, forming the lake. The sirens were always blamed for any missing people or animals.

From Pomacochas, I joined up with two guys and we went to San Martín, crossing the jungle. It took us 15 days on foot to make that trip. One night we slept along the Serranoyacu River, the river that divides the mountains from the jungle, in a house made of wood that had been built by and for travelers.

We continued our trip crossing the mountains with a three-hour hike up the mountain. Then we descended into the jungle. We arrived at a place called Aguas Verdes and slept in a camping cabin there. From that place, we caught a shortcut to the main road into the jungle. We snuck under some empty oil and gas drums in a truck and caught a ride avoiding all the military check points, making our way to Moyobamba.

In Moyobamba, we didn't have anywhere to live. One guy found an abandoned house to stay in, so we lived there with him. We didn't have food. We would go out during the day and steal corn, yucca, squash, bananas and chickens.

We liked living off other people's farms. One time we went out to a farm we knew wasn't being watched at night. We staked out the place and waited until the owner left for the day, then broke in and stole a pig.

Another time, we were going into a peanut farm and fell into a booby trap rigged with a shotgun. It could have killed us, but a dog tripped it before we got to it. The owner was nearby, however, and he came after us. He hollered after us to be careful because there were the same traps at every entrance to the farm.

The flying bullets of that afternoon started me thinking about leaving that life and looking for a job. We were aimless youth lacking identification or any formal registration with any government or community – like animals without owners. Transients.

Looking for Work

I decided to leave by way of the river and look for work; it was a done deal; I was ready for change. My friend was sad and upset. I walked to the port at Tahuishco where I took a boat down-river to Alto Mayo, and I never saw my partner in crime again. The boat left the port at eight in the morning and we traveled all day by river. The other travelers had brought their food for lunch on the river. Though I went hungry, for me it was a marvelous day. I had not previously appreciated God's creation – all the trees and animals and the birds' songs – as much as I did on that day.

In the afternoon we arrived at Puerto Ciego, after an eight-hour trip. Since I hadn't eaten breakfast or lunch, I got off quickly, grabbed a stalk of sugar cane and began cutting it up and chewing on it to keep my hunger away. Then I walked an hour into the forest, going along talking with some other men. It was interesting to see such huge trees.

I was feeling quite good when I arrived at the home of Jose Tiburcio Coronel – he and his wife Emelina Alarcón received me, a stranger, into their home. Later, their two sons, Segundo and Agustín, arrived and welcomed me saying, "Here you have a bed, food and work."

The work consisted of farming vegetables, planting rice, peanuts, bananas, yucca and corn. I tried hard to learn to work cutting trees to make posts but the bloodsucking mosquitoes were a plague that I could not bear. Day and night thousands of the little buggers stung me all over my body.

I was facing the reality of life: work to live.

The Coronels' was a Christian home and still is. I was surprised and afraid, really, when for the first time I heard them pray before eating. I had never heard the gospel nor known any born-again Christians. I thought they were worshipping Satan. It was very strange to me and I thought that I needed to do something to get them away from those strange ideas about the Bible and God and to get them back to the Roman Catholic Church.

I bought a Catholic Bible. When they would sing hymns, my body would tremble with fear. At night after dinner, they would invite me to read the Bible. Listening to their teachings made me feel desperate. Through the night I would pray to the Virgin Mary to help me keep from being fooled by the evangelicals. I would always muddle things up with a bunch of questions whenever they would try to explain the gospel to me. Always, I would praise the Catholic Church.

Sometimes I would try to act like I was asleep so I wouldn't have to hear their teachings about the Word of God. One time they invited me to a church service, but I refused and then they didn't invite me any more.

I ended up hanging out with some other foolish young kid like myself and we planned how to destroy the place where the born-again Christians worshiped. Their church was made of rustic wood and had a palm-leaf roof.

We organized a sports club and we invited the Christians to join, thinking that they might leave Jesus for soccer, but it didn't happen. Those Christians used the sport as a way of talking to us about Jesus and asking us to repent of our sins.

Those brothers peacefully responded to me in love, patience and tenderness. One night they showed me the story of the life of Joseph; it made a huge impression on me and most greatly impacted my life – I now love to read it and I get excited telling it.

A Different Family — A Lot of Love

The Coronel/Alarcón family had a very rickety house. The roof was of palm leaves and the walls of wooden poles. Instead of a mattress to sleep on we had rice straw. Despite this, they demonstrated love from their hearts toward others and it was obvious they were different from other people. Brother Jose had two teenage sons with whom I enjoyed laughing and playing. Those two young men prayed fervently to the Lord. There were also two children who were always bugging me to pick them up and carry them — Ela and Elías. Then there was Berna, the sister who was always helping their grandmother.

The family gave me the financial support that I needed to buy clothes, shoes, work tools and medicine — and besides that, they allotted me 30 hectares of land (a hectare equals about two and a half acres) to work so I could have my own land. They helped me study first aid. I did my practicum in the Regional Hospital of Moyobamba, and I came back with medicine to use in my work with the community.

Brother Jose had two single sisters: Clemencia and Clemira. One day they came to Brother Jose's house and invited me to attend a meeting. I didn't have anyone to talk to at night except the family I lived with. In the jungle you just listen to birds' caws and screeches and the other animals of the forest. Out of boredom and some interest in the girls, I decided to visit the church one night to chat and become friends with these two single sisters, since they were the only available girls in the whole place. I went with Brother Jose to the meeting every night for one week. After that week, Clemencia gave me a hymn book to sing from, but I was embarrassed to sing. Later, I bought a Protestant Bible to read together with the rest of

the congregation, but whenever asked, my beliefs were still in op-
position to Christianity.

Almost everyone there was Christian, and I couldn't escape! Sister Emelina thought my situation was humorous because I could-
n't get away from good influences – there was nowhere to go!

The Church Fasts and Prays for Narciso Zamora

The church began to form prayer chains for Narciso Zamora, for
me to come to know Jesus. They also held fasts and prayer vigils to
ask God for me to surrender my life to Christ. I thought they were
wrong for that – wasting their time. "I'm Catholic and that's how
I'll die!" I would tell them. Actually, I didn't even know what it
meant to be Catholic; I was spiritually ignorant.

To this day, I don't understand how God put it on the hearts of
those brothers to pray for me. The important element was their per-
severance in prayer. After one month of "faithfully" attending the
services, God touched my heart and opened my eyes. The Word of
God began to work and I began to take an interest in it.

I attended those services for months and I began to love the Word
of God. I would wait anxiously all afternoon for the evening message, and I wanted the hour for church service to come quickly.

The songs were not as important to me as the Word of God.
When the preacher would start to wrap up his sermon, I would
plead for a half-hour more; I needed it. I was never satisfied and always hungry for the words of Christ – there was nothing quite like
them.

One night they invited me to accept Jesus as my Savior. I told
them I still wasn't ready. I had already stopped smoking, I wasn't interested in going to dances – my life was changing and I wasn't
even realizing it. Nine months went by and I was committed to attending church during that time even though I was not a Christian.
God was working in my life. Finally, I decided that at the next opportunity that the brothers gave me to accept Christ, I would do it
and not lose any more time.

In June 1976, a missionary named Omega Vega Ríos arrived and she invited us to come for four days to their church. Sunday school started on June 6th at 10:00 a.m. The missionary preached and presented a Bible lesson and she taught us some beautiful choruses that I have not forgotten. They were: "Put Your Hand in the Hand of the Man from Galilee," "Where is the First Church?" and "I Praise Him with My Heart; I Praise Him with My Voice."

At noon that day, Sister Omega invited me to accept the Lord Jesus as my Savior and with great joy I said to her, "Yes, I want to give my life to Jesus." I went up to the front and got on my knees on the humid dirt floor. After praying together, all the brothers hugged me and that day there was a big party for everyone. I was very happy and joyful.

One of the brothers told me, "We're brothers now, glory to God." It was the happiest day of my life, and I will never forget it.

My First Course in Discipleship

The person in charge of the church, Brother Delforio Coronel, invited the youth to take a course in discipleship to prepare for baptism. Clemencia, Agustín and Segundo Coronel and I studied the Bible lessons for one month. On August 4, 1976, what I so desired came to pass.

The church in Moyobamba invited us to a seminar that lasted one week and the topics were: Principles of Biblical Doctrine, Ecclesiastic Rules of the Assemblies of God and How to Interpret the Bible. At the end of that seminar, seven of us were baptized in the Alto Mayo River.

Omega Vega, the missionary, delegated Brother Santiago Chávez to baptize us after some praise choruses and a few words by Pastor Victor Laguna. We went into the water and in the moment that I was immersed in the water I praised God and was very happy for completing this Biblical ordination and for fulfilling the commandment of the Lord. I understood that I was now a true Christian.

Afterwards, every Saturday I would travel from our community within the jungle to Moyobamba to participate in the Saturday services with the youth and Sunday school on Sunday. Then we went to the jail to hold a service in the afternoon and in the evening, there was a praise service in the church.

I took a boat back on Monday and as we traveled down river, I talked about the Word of God with people on the boat, giving them tracts while testifying of the love of Jesus.

≈

I Peter 1:7. "These have come so that your faith – of greater worth than gold, which perishes even though refined by fire – may be proved genuine and may result in praise, glory and honor when Jesus Christ is revealed."

In the small congregation in the woods, some of the deacons in the Church of Buenos Aires had started a rumor against Sister Emelina and me. Within a few days, all the farmers were talking about it and we were being branded as immoral.

I respected Sister Emelina like a mother and Brother Jose Tiburcio as a father. They were my spiritual parents; they had helped me economically and spiritually; they had given me room and board in their house.

Brother Jose told me, "The devil wants to destroy us, but he can't."

The inexperienced church leader ended up making the situation worse rather than defusing it. Soon, the situation culminated in Brother Jose getting a pistol and going after the man who had started the rumor. The moment I saw him pass by, I ducked into the sugar cane field I was standing next to, got down on my knees and began to cry out to the Lord Jesus in prayer asking God to send peace. That morning in that field, the glory of God descended on me and God touched me with his Holy Spirit. The fire of the Lord ran through me and a passion for lost souls came upon me. I knew I must leave and show the Word of God to others and preach it – even though I didn't know what that would entail. The voice of God was calling me to spread the good news of the gospel. I stayed a while longer in prayer in the field before getting up.

Thank God no one was shot that day and the next morning I

left for Moyobamba with a letter signed by the civil authorities of the community to present at court a complaint against those who had slandered me. Brother Jose had signed the letter after breakfast when he learned I was going to make the trip.

The persons who had started the rumors learned of my plans and came to ask forgiveness. They got on their knees on the floor and said it had all been a lie. The gossip had been very damaging to all involved; I didn't know how to respond. How could I forgive them?

I went on my way as planned and went first to the pastor's house in Moyobamba. I ran into and spoke with Omega Vega, the missionary. I showed her the letter I was carrying to file a complaint against the offenders. She took the letter and tore it up into four pieces. I was stunned and just glared at her with shock.

Seeing my expression, she said, "Christians don't go to the courts for judgment." She hugged me, prayed with me and invited me to stay the week for church services. It was a marvelous experience – praying and singing and learning about the word of God each day.

When I went back home, everything was smoothed over. We forgave the guilty parties and we just continued in the way of the Lord. I had peace and joy and a newfound responsibility for lost souls. It was my first Christian experience, my first trial. James said, "Resist the devil and he will flee from you."

Discussion Primers

Does Narciso's admission of delinquency in his youth weaken his credibility as a missionary? Describe a time when you were "wandering."

Who were the good influences in your life? How did your life specifically change when you first met Christ as your Savior?

What to Do for Jesus Christ?

What should I do for the Lord Jesus? The church in the community of Buenos Aires elected me to the office of secretary. I had only been a Christian for four months when the person in charge of the church asked me to preach. That seemed impossible to me, as I had no basic knowledge of how to deliver a sermon. Despite that, I accepted the invitation to give the message one Saturday night. I had in my hands a newsletter called *El Mensajero de Esperanza* (*The Faith Messenger*), from an organization in Corpus Christi, Texas, and I took advantage of it, read it and got some ideas from the text. I took a pencil and paper and wrote down what was in my heart.

Finally, the day arrived. I went up to the pulpit and read the message that I had prepared. It was the first time I ever tried to preach the word of God.

〰

We decided to build a new church, improving greatly on the little house in which we met that had spider webs and was termite-eaten. There were seven men in the effort. We each had to cut wood and palm leaves, bring them in from the woods and place them where we were going to build the new church.

One rainy afternoon, I went into the jungle to get the palm branches and leaves that I needed to build the roof of the church. I gathered a large amount of leaves and tied them together, working on the jungle floor. Suddenly, I felt a prick of what seemed to be a thorn. I let the leaves go, looked at my hand and realized that a Conga ant was attached to my right hand. I shook it loose and cut its head off with my machete. I quickly gathered the leaves and went on back to Brother Jose's house and told him that I had been bitten by a Conga ant.

They quickly gave me a shot to reduce the fever and pain that had already set in. An inexplicable, intense pain lasted 48 hours – my chest, head and underarms all ached and then the pain spread to my groin and I had a very high fever.

〰

After much hard work, we finished construction of the church. Brothers Jose and Raquel made a pulpit and the pews from cedar. In that church we had prayer meetings, vigils and days of fasting and prayer: The Lord was glorified.

The members of the church agreed to organize a special program for Christmas and the responsibility fell on me. We had agreed to spend the holiday together as a Christian family. Brother Jose prepared some special musical numbers, games and choruses; otherwise, they left the planning of the program to me.

As December began, I did not feel well physically. I was running a fever every day, which at first I thought might be a cold or flu, but then it lasted longer than 10 days and with each day my health seemed to be deteriorating more. I had yellow fever. After 15 days I couldn't even move and I lost consciousness as a result of the high fever. Brother Jose gave me daily injections of medicine and Sister Emelina prepared herbal teas and vegetable soup. I really couldn't eat, though, as my body was so weak. The fever would not let up.

I thought I would die at any moment. The brothers prayed for me and Christmas came and went and I could not even stand. But then in January 1977, God lifted me up. After one month of infirmity, my body trembling, I lifted my eyes to look around and everything got dark. But God had healed me. Brother Jose continued to give me B-12 and calcium shots and my condition improved.

When I was stronger, we went into the jungle to hunt. I learned a lot of marvelous things in that place. Later, with the help of the Coronel/Alarcon family, I was able to acquire a 15-hectare property with fruit plants and virgin forest for harvesting.

Accidents in the Jungle

Brother Jose and I were first responders to that small Amazon community and in my months there, in addition to my own illnesses, I witnessed many others that were quite serious and made a lasting impression on me.

A young man had gone out to finish chopping down some trees he had left to clear a piece of land with an axe over his shoulder, machete and shotgun in hand. He had only been working about 30 minutes when a tree fell on his leg and broke it under the knee.

When we learned of this injury, we went running out with a tetanus injection and another medication that clots the blood. The young man's leg was all but torn off. We saw exposed bone and torn flesh from which blood was pouring profusely. We did what we could and then transferred him to a hospital on a skid. He ended up losing that leg from the knee down and now has a prosthetic limb.

Another incident occurred one night when it had been raining a lot and the rivers had swelled. We heard a voice screaming from the hills, "Don Tiburcio! Help! I need help; my children are dying! Please save us!"

Fifteen days earlier, this same family, the Tapias, had lost their head of household, Alfredo Tapia, in an accident. Alfredo had drowned in the Alto Mayo River. On the night we heard the screams, all of the family members were together because of the memorial activities.

Alfredo's two sons ages 12 and 13 had been on their way home from school the day before and had picked some fruit that was just off the road. Unfortunately, the fruit was poisonous and that night around midnight, the poison had taken effect and swelled their airways to the point where they were suffocating. They were foaming at the mouth and their skin was purple. Brother Jose and I went to their aid bringing some medicinal drops, injections and pills – all the antidotes to plant and animal poisons we had – but it was too late. The oldest son had died just before we arrived and the younger was breathing very slowly in his final moments. We were able to administer some drops and decided to try to take him to a hospital.

Brother Jose carried the older son who had died and I carried the younger child and we set out in the pouring rain through the jungle forest, walking to the river port to make an emergency trip to Moyobamba. After walking about one kilometer, the boy who I was carrying on my back forcefully stretched himself out, breathed a heavy sigh, and died.

I started yelling, "The child has died!" His mother and sister dropped there in the mud and started desperately crying.

In shock and exhaustion, trudging through the rain, we continued on and carried the boys to the port and put them in a boat that the family rented to take them to the morgue in Moyobamba. We got the necessary papers from the local authorities so the family would not have a problem with the hospital authorities.

That was hard proof of the power of nature. After all that had happened – the accident with the man chopping wood, the death of Alfredo (for whose body we searched the river for three days) and later witnessing the death of those two innocent boys – to be quite honest, I revered, if not feared, the Amazon jungle.

A Great Day of Decision

In February, I decided to leave for Lima, the capital of Peru, to study in the Bible Institute to better serve my Lord Jesus. I would also take advantage of the trip to visit my parents and tell them about Jesus. I told the church about my plans and asked for prayer.

When it was time to leave, my heart ached as I hugged my brothers in Christ and started the one-hour trip to the river port. As I came near the water, I heard the sound of a motor and I looked in the distance for a boat. I saw a small boat with a tin roof coming. I signaled to its driver and he stopped. As I got on the boat, my eyes filled with tears at the thought of leaving that place which was so special to me. I was leaving the land where I met Jesus, the King of kings and Lord of lords.

After an eight-hour cruise up the river Mayo, I arrived in

Moyobamba at the pastor's house where the missionary Omega Vega lived. I stayed the night there and asked her to pray for the decision I'd made to study at the Bible Institute in Lima and for my trip. Sister Vega gave me a lot of good advice that I needed.

I left by car the next morning for Rioja where I bought a ticket for a plane that would arrive from Tarapoto. I boarded the plane and an hour later, we were in Chiclayo. The next day, I set off for Santa Cruz to visit my parents and tell them about Jesus, the Savior of the world. I traveled by truck the whole day, stayed the night in a town and the next day set off for an eight-hour walk home. I arrived home in the afternoon – very wet with sweat.

〰〰

I broke the news to my family: I was a Christian. They were not happy and that first night was awkward.

The next morning I began to sing some hymns. The neighbors started spreading gossip that a devil had come to the house of Don Marcial. My parents and siblings told me, "They say Christians worship the devil and goats." No one appreciated my decision; they made fun of me. They also said, "Evangelicals are Moors," which they meant as an insult. My spirit was wounded, but I tried not to let it get to me.

I decided I should leave home quickly and I did – walking through the mountains singing and praising the Lord and carrying a package of tracts. I arrived at a small mining town called Hualgayoc, which is 3,000 meters above sea level. I stayed the night there and the next day went on toward Cajamarca by bus.

On the bus, I made use of my captive audience to pass out the tracts I had on hand. One man came up to me later and asked me a lot of questions then preached a little sermon to me! He was a Jehovah's Witness. I just told him what Jesus had done in my life.

That afternoon we arrived in Cajamarca and I went directly to the Rose of Sharon Church. The pastor there gave me some written information about the Bible Institute in Lima and I grew excited about studying theology.

The pastor told me, "I'll be praying for you; prepare yourself to serve the Lord Jesus."

Once in Lima, I went to my uncle's house and spent one week there. I told them I had become a born-again Christian and as soon as the words left my mouth, their reception toward me changed and chilled. They said they didn't like having born-again Christians in their house because they believed that Christians adored Satan. The Catholics, on the other hand, with all their statues hung in their cathedrals, churches and houses, adored saints.

While with my uncles, I had the opportunity to see my younger brother, Orlando. He walked with crutches after having spent four years in a medical care home. I had always loved my brother a lot and still do and was so glad to see him. I talked with him at length to see if he would like to continue his studies so he could finish high school. He said he would like that. We enrolled him in a high school near the house where he was living and I bought his uniform and school supplies. He went daily to school, aided by a crutch.

Content knowing that my brother was well and going to continue his education, I had to take care of myself by finding a place to live, perhaps in some evangelical church, I thought.

Early one Sunday morning, with my packed suitcase and no idea of where I would end up, I walked through the dusty streets of a neighborhood in Lima known as El Callao, looking for an evangelical church that might take me in. It was a couple of hours later when I spotted a man with a broom standing next to the path.

I stopped and asked him, "Do you know where an evangelical church might be?"

He replied, "This is one."

I was so happy. I told him all my problems and started crying because of the rejection I had felt from my family.

The brother said, "You can stay here. We'll give you a room to sleep in."

I gladly accepted the offer. Now I had a place to sleep but something I didn't have was a way to satisfy my hunger. I went 25 days without food, drinking only water.

I went out looking for work in different places throughout Lima.

One day I had been out walking all day looking for a job. I sat down to take a rest on a park bench and I lifted my eyes to look up at the buildings and everything went black – I couldn't see. I fell over and off the bench; I couldn't get up.

At yet another extremely low moment, I cursed the gospel because my friends and family had rejected me because I was a Christian. I thought I would have been better off dying in the jungle and I asked myself, "Why am I here in Lima?" I didn't have anything to eat, I couldn't find work, and I had no money. What should I do? As I was struggling in that agony, I looked up and saw a sign in front of me that said, "The Story of Moses." I stopped and looked at it then began to walk toward it. The sign was for a movie theater that was showing the film "The Ten Commandments." I blended in with a group of people who were walking in to see the film and I was able to sneak into the theater. After watching the story of Moses, his struggles and victory through the Lord, I fell down on my knees and asked the Lord to forgive me, saying, "Help me, Lord!"

The next day, I went to the Bible Institute in El Callao, an area in Lima. They gave me some enrollment forms to fill out and bring back to the secretary before an interview with the director. As I was leaving, the assistant director told me, "Come back a week from now and we'll see if you're accepted into the program. Then we'll tell you what you must do from there."

A week went by; I went back and the secretary, Sister Maria Sandoval, told me, "Very well, Brother Narciso, the director has accepted your application and you may enroll."

What a joy it was for me to find out that I had been accepted to study theology. But I had a problem: I did not have the money that I needed to enroll, buy books or pay my room and board.

I ran into Pedro Dávila, my father's first cousin, and I told him that I really wanted to study theology and that I'd been accepted for enrollment.

He said, "Congratulations, Nephew," and then loaned me 300 sols with which to start my studies.

His words and financial support greatly encouraged me.

Welcome to Class

One week later, I started school at the Bible Institute – April 1, 1977. There were 35 first-year students who started classes together. That same afternoon after classes, I walked down Faucett Avenue looking for work and found a job in a melting pot factory. The pots, or crucibles, were made for testing lead in the labs of mining centers. I studied during the day and I worked in the afternoon.

The result of my efforts: I soon came down with tuberculosis. My fellow students prayed for me and for another student, Moya, who suffered as well. God in his mercy restored my health. My friend Moya, however, had to return to his home in Cuzco due to his case of tuberculosis.

After I had worked my job about two months, one of my professors, a missionary named Gene Steel, and his wife Betty, asked me to stay late after my class of systematic theology. They told me, "Brother Narciso, we would like to talk to you."

We went in their car to downtown Lima for lunch at a place on the corner of Nicolás de Piérola, in front of the Plaza San Martín. It was a nice restaurant. As we were eating, Professor Steel said, "I would like to help you by paying two months of your room and board, but my condition is that you leave your job. God will supply your needs."

I did as my professor advised, I quit my job and I began living at the Bible Institute.

〜

The daily schedule of the Bible Institute was quite strict and rigorous. The bell rang at 5:30 a.m. for us to wake up and wash up, and then we were to pray for 40 minutes. At 6:10 a.m., the bell rang again for us to do our chores, which involved the upkeep of the facility, such as cleaning the restrooms, chapel, offices, dining room, kitchen, etc. When the bell rang again, we would leave our brooms and cleaning supplies, wash our hands and make a single-file line for breakfast – all the men through the north door and the women through the south door.

Breakfast consisted of a cup of milk with oatmeal and a banana and we had 15 minutes to eat. We then changed into our uniforms, a suit and tie, to be ready to start class. Those assigned to kitchen duty for the week had to finish cleaning the kitchen and wash all the dishes, pots and pans.

At 7:00 a.m. the professor for our first class would call roll. Between our classes, at 9:00 a.m., we went to chapel for devotions. They used this hour as a practicum for second and third year students. As they spoke, they were graded on diction, grammar and sermon delivery. At 10:00 a.m. we went back to the classroom to continue our studies until the afternoon. When the afternoon bell rang, we left class, returned to our rooms, left our books there, changed out of our uniforms and went to the dining room for lunch.

We lined up the same as during breakfast and always with a tray in our hands to receive our food. We had one hour for a casual lunch with conversation. Lunch consisted of a vegetable soup and a second plate with rice and either fish, spaghetti or sweet potato – that was the menu every day except for Sunday when we had vegetables, chicken and noodles. After our lunch hour, we had more chores to do, including cleaning the buildings and working in the garden, painting walls, etc. The women would clean and prepare the vegetables for the next days' meals and finish cleaning any pots and pans.

At 5:00 p.m. the dinner bell rang and we took our cue again with trays in hand. After dinner, at 7:00 p.m., the third-year students would gather to study and do homework. Others would go to the library.

At 9:45 p.m. a final bell rang and all the students gathered in a common room, some to talk, others to laugh a little or have coffee. At 10:00 p.m. it was to our beds and lights out.

We studied from Monday to Saturday without days off or holidays. On Sunday, we all went to church, some to preach, others to teach Sunday school and others to evangelize in the area.

While classes were in session, we had no holidays or breaks. On Sundays the students went out into churches. The school administrators gave us a form to fill out listing the different outside activities in which we were involved on Sundays. The pastor of the church that we attended on Sunday signed the form. We had to turn it in to the secretary on Sunday night or Monday morning.

~~~

My school had an unusual ritual. Starting at 11:00 p.m., on any night, one male student after another would make his way in silent procession from the bedrooms to "the lodgings," which was about 90 meters away. "The lodgings" was a small, old house and all night long students would go there to kneel and pray. Some would enter as others were exiting. Men cried and called out to the Lord in that place. We each had a lot of needs and many a student on bended knee on the lodgings' wide wooden bench had a real encounter with Jesus.

The two months that Professor Steel had paid for me passed and I didn't have any money to continue paying for my room and board and there was no one to help me pay and no one I even dared ask. That's when I sought out the lodgings – that place of heart-wrenching sobs and pleas – and for the rest of my three years, I went there to cry to the Lord and call on him to supply my needs. I poured my heart out asking for God's help.

My needs were pressing, as a debt was accumulating.

I decided to ask the director to be allowed to leave for three hours each day in the afternoon to sell magazines and books in downtown Lima. I walked through the streets and went into restaurants to offer my wares to the people dining. Though some days I was blessed, other days I sold nothing, and that worried me. What to do? I set up a little stand on the corner of Emancipation Avenue and Abancay and I would offer books and magazine for sale to people passing by.

When the school year ended, I was in debt for three months tuition, room and board. The director called me to his office. I was shaking as I walked in wondering what to say to him.

He said, "Brother Zamora, you are eating the food that belongs to the other young students. When will you pay your bill? Or do you want to leave the Bible Institute; the doors are open."

I asked him to have patience and told him I would soon pay the bill. I was ashamed but I badly wanted to continue my studies.

During our break, I traveled into the Andean Mountains of Peru to a mining center called Raura, located about 4,000 meters above sea level. For two months, I helped the church there and God blessed me greatly. I was able to return to the Bible Institute when classes started again and I went into the office and paid my entire debt and paid for three months in advance.

The Director, Reverend Ernesto Sandoval, congratulated me and said, "May God help you to continue on."

Spring Break, Seminary Style

Sister Omega Vega, one of my spiritual mothers, helped me pay for four more months that year — tuition, room and board and books. When I received the money, I immediately wrote thanking her and asking her to write me back. For the rest of 1978, I didn't hear from her.

I was happy when December break rolled around and we left for Christmas vacation. I went out with literature to sell. I traveled to different churches along the northern coast of Peru. I was able to preach in some of the churches. I then traveled into the Amazon jungle region to visit my Christian family where I had received Christ. When I arrived there in January 1979, Brother Jose was very happy to see me and welcomed me. I stayed there one month. God used me in a marvelous way while I was there — several souls came to know Jesus as their personal Savior.

I preached in churches and homes, outdoors in parks. I saw people kneeling to accept Jesus as God used his Word in a great way. I was very grateful to God.

During that same break, in February I traveled for the first time to visit the Aguaruna tribe in San Rafael, Morroyacu and Shimpiy-acu. Brother Delforio Coronel and I started out on the trip one morning at 5 a.m. loaded with machete, shotgun, bedrolls, a cooking pot, sugar, matches and mosquito nets. There was no road to walk on most of the way — just a hunting trail. The trees in the jungle were gigantic — some as big as 50 meters tall producing such a thick cover that we couldn't see the sun.

We walked until 5:00 in the afternoon that first day and were tired. We stopped and made our beds. We used palm leaves woven in tree branches about three meters above us to form a sort of house and inside we placed palm leaves on the foundation, our blankets and mosquito nets hanging just above our "beds." Below on the jungle floor animals were moving about all night long and many of them were savage beasts. Brother Delforio was ready all night with his flashlight and shotgun.

At 5:00 in the morning, we started to pack up and resume the hike. We came down out of the trees and lit a fire to make breakfast which consisted of corn cakes. A turkey Brother Delforio shot served as meat for our lunch.

The second day we made it as far as the Yurayacu River. Brother Delforio said, "I believe we must be getting close." Throughout the entire hike we had many faithful companions in the mosquitoes — they were like a black cloud following us. There were also many parrots and other birds, monkeys, wild turkeys and snakes. The snakes got up to three inches in diameter and nine feet long. Brother Delforio killed those with his shotgun.

At 3:30 that afternoon we arrived at Morroyacu, a village of Aguaruna natives consisting of about a dozen happy families. When we entered the clearing where the village stood, it was our first time to see the sun in two days because we had been under the thick jungle canopy. As we walked into the village, everyone ran and hid — men, women and children — only one short man came out to welcome us. His name was Haches and he was the leader of the tribe.

〜〜〜

We were so thankful to God when we reached that first tribe, the leader came out to greet us and he held in his hands a horn, and blowing through it, called the whole community together to listen to the message of God. After he blew his horn, he ushered us into a house and gave us a log to sit on and invited us to partake of some mazato. It is a juice made of yuca ground on a trunk. To ferment it, the women chew the yuca and spit it into an earthen jar. The chewing accelerates the fermentation. They serve it in small clay cups. This was the first test: If we drank this, we would be welcome there. Mazato is very bitter, ask me how I know.

After a successful visit, we left that community accompanied by the leader of the tribe. We crossed the river and one hour later we arrived at the Shimpiyacu village. Another short man received us, the leader of this second Aguaruna community. He then called his tribe with a horn that resembled a trumpet. With the horn he could let them all know, regardless of where they were, of our arrival. We rested there that night and the next day; we preached and showed them the Word of God. The tribe suspended all of their regular activities to listen and that entire tribe accepted Jesus as their Savior.

In the brief time I was with the natives, I could not discern any regular work or eating schedule. It seemed a person could eat when they wanted and however much they felt like eating – smoked meats and roasted fruit all day. There were no eating utensils or a dining room. People just ate.

The Aguaruna hunt their meat with blowguns. They are made from long, hollowed branches – sometimes two pieces with a channel cut down the center then bound together. They use very thin wooden darts, the points of which they wrap with a sort of cotton that is dipped in curare poison. When they spot their prey, they aim and blow forcefully and if the dart pierces the animal, it will be poisoned within seconds and then die. Within a few hours, the poison dissolves and the meat is then no longer dangerous to eat. The Aguaruna start cooking fires by rubbing wood together so long and forcefully that sparks jump and start a fire. To chase away the mosquitoes, the Aguaruna keep a fire going all night on a very large tree trunk that will burn slowly, mostly smoking. A smoking tree inside the house enables them to sleep free of mosquitoes.

I learned many fascinating things about those master survivors.

And from us, they learned of God's Son, Jesus. Three tribal villages accepted Jesus: Shimpiyacu, Morroyacu and San Raphael. For one week, I preached and we had Bible classes with the tribe, teaching them to pray and sing praises to God. Below is the chorus "Jesus Loves Me" in the language of the Aguaruna:

"Tatayusa Mina Anentui"	"Jesus Loves Me"
Dega Tatayusa mina anentui	Yes, Jesus loves me
Dega Tatayusa mina anentui	Yes, Jesus loves me
Dega Tatayusa mina anentui	Yes, Jesus loves me
Tatayusa chichame tawai atus.	The Bible tells me so.

This was the first chorus the Aguarunas learned. I was over-whelmed at seeing the people of the tribe accept Christ, all of them on their knees, from the very old who wore clothes to the very young who were perfectly content in pure nakedness. All were kneeling and praying to accept Christ. It was a wonder.

〜〜

Brother Delforio and I left and headed back to Buenos Aires where we participated in some church activities before heading out to Tarapoto to meet with a small congregation from the Assemblies of God. We spent several days preaching there. The church members generously bought my ticket to travel back to Lima to resume my studies in the Bible Institute.

That final year while I studied, I pastored a small congregation in Carabayllo, which is about 18 kilometers north of Lima. In the morning I studied at the Bible Institute and in the afternoon, I went to my church to work in the ministry.

Discussion Primers

Contemplate this statement in relation to God's power: "…I revered, if not feared, the Amazon jungle."

Narciso's decision to become an evangelical Christian is not welcomed in his family. Describe a time when a close personal relationship was in jeopardy because of your Christianity. What does "...prepare yourself to serve the Lord Jesus" mean to you?

What is the tone with which Narciso describes his experiences with the Aguarunas, or the "natives?" How is it similar or distinct to your impression, t this point, of the culture in which Narciso lives?

A Year of Decision

It was my last year in the Bible Institute — classes and my "practicum" as minister in Carabayllo had come to fulfillment. That experience helped me greatly and changed my life. I met a very special person named Udelia.

Udelia had two children, a 10-year-old and a 12-year-old, and every weekend they would invite me to have lunch at their house. It was completely innocent for me because at that time, I was seeing another young lady, an accounting student. However, after she finished her studies, her father wanted her to return home to a city in the north of Peru. She went and our relationship became a long-distance romance — writing letters and once every three months she would come back to Lima and we would see each other for a weekend. But it soon fizzled out.

From that point on, I found myself spending more time with Udelia. I looked on her as a very respectable woman because she had two children and she was older than I. One day we were horsing around and we clasped hands. That moment changed the way I saw her and from then on, we started to grow closer all the way to the day we got married.

I asked Udelia about her children, where the father was, who the father was. She told me she was a widow and that settled the issue for me. Udelia lived with two elderly uncles who were raising her children as if they were their own — the kids even called them "Papa" and those men were really responsible for all the opportunities those kids had later on.

When Udelia and I married, the uncles didn't want to let the children go with us to the jungle to pastor a church. They needed the children to help take care of them — do the cooking and clean the house. We left the kids with the uncles in Lima where they were enrolled in private schools and then went on to higher education. Once a year, Udelia would make a trip home to see her children.

Years later I learned the sad truth about Udelia's two children and why it was possible for her to leave them and travel with me.

~~~

My graduation was in December 1979 and Sister Omega Vega sent me the equivalent of $15 to buy a suit for graduation. It was the first new suit I had ever owned. During my three years as a student, I had always worn a second-hand suit and some shoes that a Christian couple had given me. I took very good care of them and they had lasted the entire three years.

As December neared, I was so excited to be graduating and realizing a goal. It was such a privilege to don a cap and gown – our color was burgundy.

Many of the churches in Lima were invited. The sports field where the graduation took place was full of people. The procession of students was in this order: first-year students, second-year students and finally the graduates. Sister Isolina de Sandoval, the music director, started the program with some songs, prayer, a scripture reading and a special number by the Institute's choir. The theme was "Missionary Fire" and the choir's selection fit it well. One of the students gave the message from the Word of God.

The adrenaline in my body left me numb, my heart was beating so fast – I was about to graduate.

Ernesto Sandoval, the director, came up to the podium and after some encouraging words, the graduates began to file past him in alphabetical order. He took our tassels and in the name of the Father, the Son and the Holy Spirit, turned them to graduate us and then gave us our diploma. Victory in Jesus!

When the ceremony ended, I spotted my wife in the huge crowd and another couple coming up to me to congratulate me. The couple was my Uncle Pedro Dávila and his wife. Uncle Pedro was the man who had loaned me 300 soles to start my studies. I hadn't seen them in three years. They hugged me and after taking some photos, we left.

My Uncle Pedro had a surprise for me. We took a taxi to Avenida Alfonso Ugarte in Lima and he treated my wife and me to an elegant dinner in a restaurant. It was like a banquet and so exciting. My uncle said, "That was the first time I have ever attended an evangelical Christian function and the first graduation like that I've ever seen in my life. It was a beautiful ceremony; I really enjoyed it. You looked like Martin Luther up there."

At that moment, I felt ready for battle. The day, topped off with my Uncle Pedro's attendance and attention, put me on top of the mountain.

The next day I went back to say good-bye to all my friends and the faithful brothers of my studies. We were all heading out now to fight the great fight to win souls for Christ. Almost 30 years have passed and I never saw any of those friends again. I pray that God has continued to bless the work to which he called each of us.

I left the church in Carabayllo to start a new church in Collique, a town not too far away. My wife joined me in this work as did Brother Stefano Palmisano, an Italian preacher and World War II veteran. In just a short time, God blessed us with a congregation.

We planned a camp meeting to grow the work. One Saturday night during that effort, we stayed away from home all night and while we were gone, thugs broke into our house and carried away all we owned – presumably with a truck. Dining room, kitchen, living room and bedrooms – they took everything. In one complete blow we were left with nothing.

The next day, after Sunday evening service, we arrived home and were shocked to find an empty house. Our neighbors loaned us some blankets to sleep with that night. We got on our knees in prayer that night and told the Lord all that had happened to us. It was a hard thing, sad and very difficult to accept.

〰

The Assemblies of God church in Tarapoto in the Amazon

invited me to be their pastor. I had been praying and waiting on the Lord to know his will and where he would have us work in his vineyard. When we found out there was a church that needed us, we had no doubts that this was God's will. We quickly put our affairs in order and packed our bags for the trip.

It was March 1980 when my wife and I left for Tarapoto. She carried with her in her womb our son, Gerson. We had to travel to Rioja in a truck that was hauling vegetables. We had taken a mat with us to be able to lay down on the trip and rest. We took turns, one sitting up with the driver and the other lying on the mat in the back. Five days and five nights we traveled in that truck.

Extremely tired, we arrived in Rioja at 7:00 one evening. It was dark already and the driver took us to the home of Percy Quiroz, an officer in the national police force. His wife Maria received us into her home. We chatted with the officer and participated that night in a service within the home.

The next day, we continued our trip to Tarapoto in a small truck and arrived mid-afternoon. My wife stayed in the marketplace watching our things while I went to look for Jose Martinez Encinas, our correspondent.

We went to get Udelia, and Brother Martinez took us back to his home and gave us lodging for one week with them while we found someplace to live. A young man named Segundo Shalamaus rented us a small house that hadn't been lived in for a while. We had to rid it of cobwebs before we could move in.

In that place, my wife had to take up her cross with the mosquitoes. She cried daily because she was being eaten alive with bites all over her legs and arms. We hung a mosquito net over our beds to enable us to sleep at night. Besides those buggers, we had to deal with lots of spiders and lizards running all around the house in a balmy 38° Celsius – a temperature which stayed constant day and night.

The church was small with only 11 adults – no young people – but it did have some young children. They offered us a stipend of 16,000 soles monthly, a wage much lower than the minimum for that time. God would have to sustain us, or so we believed. We accepted the job and began the work with fasting and prayer.

A group of us went out into the jungle about an hour's walk to a hut that belonged to one Brother Gilbert. He let us stay there. We were going to have a retreat of sorts. We arrived around 9:00 in the morning and immediately began our work of prayer, singing and worshiping the Lord and searching his word. We stayed there two days in fasting and prayer and while we were there, we had some mysterious and threatening experiences unlike anything I've witnessed before or since in my ministry.

We asked our first deacon of the church, Brother Jaime Gomez, the director and a teacher at the high school in a nearby town, to station himself at the door of the hut while continuing to pray. We prayed all day without stopping to rest. Around 3:00 p.m. of that first day, we began a praise service and then we went to our knees again in prayer. Suddenly, we heard a sound like rocks falling on the roof of the house. The roof was made of palm leaves so it wasn't very noisy, just bothersome.

Brother Jaime stood up to see what was happening while the group continued to pray. What he saw was a child with a large head and eyes that were too small, very thin arms and legs, like a little monster. When he looked at him, the child closed his eyes and called him; he did this twice. Brother Jaime dropped to his knees and started praying with all his might to rebuke the devil.

When the group prayer was over, Brother Jaime gave a testimony of what he had seen — a demon and it was throwing the rocks at the roof. We went to the Word of God and then repented with all our might in the name of Jesus — some were even shouting their prayer.

Time passed quickly and before we knew it, it was 10:00 p.m. Everything was peaceful and each of us was praising God in testimony. God had given us a victory. At 11:00 p.m. we decided to call it a day and part of the group went to a loft in the hut and the other part stayed below. We agreed to get up early and begin praying again, but if some wanted to sleep in, that was all right too.

Some woke as early as 5:00 a.m. and began praying right where they were sleeping. They woke me with their prayers and my wife and I both immediately joined them in prayer.

While we were praying, I had a vision. I could see a church around me and all the congregation was listening to me preach the Word of God. Suddenly, in came a black bull, and the congregation scattered. Some ran for the woods, others up to the mountains. Two brothers ran in front of me and I followed them. The bull was chasing me down a very rocky road with trees lining each side. The bull ran me off the road and I lost sight of the men I was following. Off the road, I looked up into the distance and I could see fields full of yellow wheat. I could see the marvels of God, and I forgot about everything that was happening and just began to walk toward the wheat fields. This was my vision.

When I got up from that prayer, the sun was just coming out. I started moving around preparing for our second day of fasting and prayer. I told the brothers who were with me about my vision and asked them to pray that God would clean out our church and give us the victory, because sin was damaging the church.

Everyone was surprised to hear this. "What is it?" they asked.

I started to cry and could only mutter, "Lord, give us your power to face and reject evil."

Some of the brothers had problems with the fast. They began to vomit greenish water, others seemed like they might die any minute. But we continued on united in fervent prayer until we had the victory. The sun was going down in the sky; we knew it was getting late. We looked at the clock and saw it was 4:30 p.m. We ended our prayer at 5:00 p.m. and got ready to go home.

When we finished our fast, Sister Misahua Ohaquí arrived with one of her daughters. They had brought a pot of chicken and plantain soup. We all ate and at 6:00 p.m., we went home.

My wife, who was almost ready to give birth, participated in that fast and prayer and received a great blessing, as well.

≈

One week later, one of the members of our church board caught the wife of one of our deacons in the very act of adultery with another deacon. He immediately exhorted them with scripture to repent of the sin. The woman did and said she would never do it again. He prayed for her and believed that everything would end there.

Ten days later, on one of my home visits, I caught the adulterous couple again engaged in inappropriate contact. After carefully considering the situation and some discussion, we decided the two needed to be disciplined. The board called the couple and presented them with a letter of discipline that would last an indefinite amount of time — until we could see by their testimony that they had changed — and I revoked the deacon's credentials and their membership in the church.

That same week, the leader of the church youth, a federal police officer, Brother Quiroz, found the couple again engaged in adultery. He threw them in jail for immoral acts and called us and told us what had happened.

The board met again and decided to expel the couple from the church, a decision that also met with the approval of the general church membership. The secretary prepared a letter of expulsion for each of them and we took it to each of their homes.

Three days later on a Sunday evening, the couple showed up at church, drunk and wielding a knife to kill the pastor. I was behind the pulpit when the couple entered the church. The man furiously demanded that we return his membership card to him. The congregation was frightened and the children started screaming. After a suspenseful moment of indecision, some brothers stood up and started to talk sternly with him on my behalf. Others started to pray. This man had been in jail in his youth. He had known Jesus for a while but returned to the devil. I was able to stand only with the support of the pulpit while I responded to the man's threats then began praying that the couple would do no harm.

The brothers finally talked the couple into leaving. On his way out the door, the man yelled back a threat that he would be back at 10:00 p.m. and he demanded we return his membership card at that time. I had torn up the cards and thrown them away — there was no way to give them their cards back.

As soon as the service was over, some of us began to pray on our knees. My wife was very afraid, and so was I, for that matter.

In front of the church lived a neighbor who didn't like evangelical churches. He had been a witness to all that had happened — the man entering with the knife in hand and the threats. He came to us and said, "I will help you if that criminal comes back. I'll kill him myself." He took out a gun, loaded it and was ready to shoot the offender. Those of us who had remained at church began to get very worried and we stayed inside the building.

At 11:00 p.m. Brothers Jaime Gomez and Alfonso Rios left on a motorcycle to fetch the police. While we waited in the doorway, two journalists came by on a moped to take information about what was going on. A little later, the police arrived. They had dealt with the man who was threatening us back in the days before he had accepted Christ. They said he was a dangerous criminal and they wanted to be cautious. One of the officers got his gun out and went around the church looking to see if he might be hiding. Then a boy who had been playing nearby came up to the police and told them he had seen the couple quite drunk going into a house where liquor was sold, some two blocks from a bar. With this information, the police found them, arrested them and they were jailed. The woman was released after a few hours, but the man stayed there overnight.

The next day on the front page of the newspaper, the story read "Evangelical Pastor Narciso Zamora was assaulted by a criminal who sought to attack him with a firearm inside the High Temple Room Church."

The storm was over, the devil was defeated, the sin was removed from our church and a marvelous new growth began.

We planned a project to conduct evangelism campaigns and to organize and grow our Sunday school program. Each month we had a campaign with a different speaker and musical group and we showed films. During seven months of work, the congregation grew from 11 to 68, including a good group of youth. Our Sunday school grew too. During the month of August, we baptized 17 new Christians — and though a great blessing, the baptism was the impetus of a fateful turn of events.

Judged and Condemned

The policy of the Assemblies of God Church says (paraphrased): A pastor who has graduated from seminary or a Bible institute may not conduct any ordinances or catechisms. Only ordained ministers may perform these functions, unless the presbytery has granted specific permission.

Our church wrote a letter to the presbytery, the church's governing office in our area, asking that Reverend Santiago Chavez come to perform the baptisms of our new converts and the Lord's Supper. The pastor accepted the invitation. Under direction of the church, he was to come via the Morales River which would bring him directly to the location where the baptism would take place.

On the day of the baptism, we all went to the river, taking our lunches for a picnic. The candidates for baptism were there as well. We waited until 4:00 p.m. that day and Santiago Chavez did not come. The board gathered and one of the deacons said, "Pastor Zamora, we'll take responsibility for you if you will just conduct this baptism. It's getting late and we all need to get home." The board was a little frustrated that the minister from the presbytery had not shown up.

Brother Jaime Gomez accompanied me in the baptism. It was very late by the time we finished the baptisms, and we immediately left for our houses and then ended the evening with a church service. Reverend Chavez arrived in time to oversee the Lord's Supper. I spoke to him and explained that I had conducted the baptisms since he had not come in time, well knowing that I was committing an infraction against the rules of the church by baptizing without permission. I asked him to let me explain the case to the regional directors in their next meeting.

He replied, "This is serious."

Reverend Chavez spent that night in my home. The next day my wife sewed a shirt for him. On the third day, he went back to Moyobamba.

My son, Gerson, was born on September 3, 1980, just days before the regional directors meeting; therefore, I could not attend to explain my case. I asked for an extension until the month of October.

Reverend Chavez told me not to worry.

Nonetheless, the regional directors did not grant an extension. They took up my case in the September meeting and decided to discipline me for six months by suspending me from my ministerial activities. In the second week of September, Reverend Chavez and three members of the board of regional directors came and had with them two copies of a resolution, one for me and the other for the congregation. It was written in this manner:

The regional directors are disciplining Pastor Narciso Zamora for committing an infraction of the church rules of this institution and from this date he is withdrawn from his ministry and unable to exercise any of the duties thereof for six months.

1. Brother Zamora will attend punctually all the services of the church but without vote or voice, he may only be an observer.
2. He must sit in the last pew and not participate.
3. He will tithe to the regional directors.
4. He is prohibited from visiting any of the members of the church in their homes.
5. He is not to participate in activities of other churches or denominations.

Rationale:

1. For having baptized with water without permission from the presbytery.
2. For committing an infraction of the rules of the church.
3. For rebellion in not attending the September meeting of the regional directors.
4. For assuming responsibilities rightly belonging to the presbytery.

I was very upset at receiving this resolution directly from the hands of Reverend Chavez because he had promised me that this matter would be continued until the month of October so that I could attend the directors' meeting. They had passed judgment on the crime without ever hearing the defense.

What was the real motive for that decision? In my opinion, three things were behind that series of events: ambition, retaliation and fear of losing control of the leadership.

∿

My wife cried. The church promised me they would continue to support my family and me financially. The first month they gave me the offering, I felt ashamed to be receiving it without having done any work. So my wife and I decided we would tell the church that we didn't want the offering any more and they should use it for other needs within the church. They accepted this proposal.

We were very needy, I didn't have any other work at that time and we didn't know how we would live. It was difficult. We had to leave the house we were living in and look for a cheaper one. We sold our radio, blender, pants, underwear and jackets. We worked making clothes and I went out to sell in different communities – Alto Huallaga, El Cumbre, San Jose de Sisa and Santa Cruz – sometimes by truck, other times by boat, and even by small airplane. I was gone up to four days at a time trying to sell the clothing. I traded clothes for chickens, turkeys and ducks (in some areas of the jungle, people don't use money but rather barter goods). On several occasions, I filled the small transport plane with animals on my way home from San Jose.

The school teachers in the various small towns I visited making sales calls usually gave me lodging and allowed me to conduct Bible studies in the school house. As I walked from home to home selling, families would offer me breakfast, lunch and dinner – I never had to worry about food. I carried the clothes to sell in a big suitcase and my tracts and Bible in a small pack that I kept under my arm.

On the days that I would stay in the jungle communities to sell clothes, I took the opportunity to evangelize at each home I entered. I offered my wares, and then I offered a tract and would tell the people about Jesus. I then invited them to come to the rural school house in the afternoon where I would be conducting a Bible study. I preached the gospel and many people accepted Jesus in those small communities.

As a result of those sales trips, two congregations formed in Alto Huallaga and I distributed literally thousands of tracts among the population of those jungle communities. Christian Triumph Company supplied me with boxes of tracts and hymnals.

When I would arrive home laden with animals I'd bartered for clothes, my wife would set about selling them so we could buy more material with which to make more clothes to sell. God helped us survive while using me, my wife and even my baby Gerson to reach the Peruvian jungle with the gospel. This was the will of God – that I should go out into those tiny communities along the shores of the Huallaga and Amazon Rivers. We didn't realize it at that time, though. We thought only that we were suffering and had to continue fighting to survive without sacrificing the spreading of the gospel, particularly through literature. We never took a vacation. We had no "down time." We preached without rest, going places no preacher had ever been, and the people there received the good news of Jesus Christ.

For all the work we did, we only made enough money to buy beans and plantains for ourselves. We ate that everyday, always believing that if we trusted in God, we would prosper.

A Frightening Day

One Tuesday, I left the house very early, not really knowing where I would go that day. I caught a truck toward El Cumbre and after two hours of travel, we came on a small town. The driver parked in the Plaza de Armas, the town square, and all the passengers got out and each went walking in their own direction until within just a minute or two everyone had disappeared. I squared away my bags and my backpack, threw them up on my shoulder and started to walk.

Within five minutes, I was almost out of the town. The sun was beating down hard on my back. I looked up and saw trees all around just off the road. I decided to walk through the trees for some shade and look for a house in the woods. Soon I could no longer see the road and then I found myself in a corn field that also had beans, peas and yucca. I walked a while looking for a way back into the woods. Once in the woods again, I walked for a long time and it started to get late and even grow dark and I couldn't find anything – no houses and no way out of the jungle. I saw various birds, including parrots and macaws, monkeys and snakes, slithering on the ground and hanging off of trees. I hadn't eaten all day and I was tired and started to become very afraid. I simply could not find a way out of the jungle. I climbed up a tree to see if there was a house nearby and I didn't see anything but more trees – one big green blot on the bottom and the blue sky above for as far as I could see. I paused for a moment and prayed to God to help me get out of there.

A few minutes later, I heard a rooster crow and I stopped to listen for it again. He crowed again and I was so relieved. I picked up my bags and walked in the direction of the crow. It was 6:00 p.m. when I finally got out of that jungle and could see the light of day again – with a very happy heart.

Thank God I arrived at a small community of 10 families called Nuevo Santa Cruz. I asked for lodging and even had a Bible study with the family I stayed with and one other family. The family gave me a hammock to sleep in that night because there was no other bed. Also, it's not advisable to sleep on the floor where snakes, spiders and Conga ants might roam. I stayed three days in that small community and sold all the clothes I had with me. During the day, I visited with the families and spoke about Jesus.

On the way home as I was walking again through fields and woods, rains came down strong. I was completely drenched, but when the rain let up, I let the clothes air dry on me as I walked along.

I praise the Lord Jesus for always being with me, walking at my side, glory to God. Jesus said, "I am with you always, to the very end of the age," Matthew 28:20.

The Day of Reinstatement Arrives

I was very happy as the six months of sanction drew to a close, thinking about returning to my post within the church. Yet as my wife and I prayed a prayer of dedication, we began to think the Lord might be leading us to remain in missionary work, evangelizing and planting new churches without preaching in an established church.

Because of the work I was doing during my sanction and how it required me to travel, I could not attend any meetings of the regional directors during my sanction, though I did directly send my tithes to them as I had been ordered to do. The directors had asked the church to report to them as to whether I was fulfilling the conditions of the discipline. The church told them the truth that I only attended once a week or sometimes every other week. The regional directors took this as a sign of rebellion and intentionally disregarding the conditions set forth in my discipline.

After six months was over, the presbytery opted not to lift my sanction but to leave me in that status. They sent documents to the district office and from there to the national office. When I heard this, I cried and felt very ashamed. There was no one to come to my defense, not one servant of God to encourage or give me strength to get through this.

I continued to sell clothes in nearby communities and I added plastic wares to my collections. I took a load to sell and visited Brother Jose Tiburcio.

My dear friend Jose asked me, "Brother Narciso, is it a problem to work without credentials, free from any earthly institution as long as you're serving Jesus?" It's a memory that can't be erased from my heart, seeing him there next to that contraption he was using to grind down sugar cane to make brown sugar.

I replied, "Thank you, my Brother Jose, that's what I'll do. I'm going to send my credentials back to the presbytery and work with my Lord Jesus and only for him."

I felt a little better when he gave me a hug as I left. I walked an hour with a lot of wares on my back. I hadn't sold anything and I was heading home very slowly, feeling weak and still discouraged. I had no money to take home to my family, and yet I felt I had to resign from the Assemblies of God and dedicate myself to an independent endeavor.

I went to the port to wait for a boat. I saw one approaching from far away on the Alto Mayo River. It was a rustic craft with a tin roof, full of animals, supplies and people – there were 20 of us in total running on a 16-horsepower motor. We floated very slowly down the river watching what seemed to be the trees filing by – a lovely eight hours on that rickety, crowded watercraft.

When I got to Moyobamba, I left my bags at the Coronel's house and went downtown to buy some paper and an envelope. That night I drafted a letter of resignation and I inserted my credentials in the envelope.

Early the next morning I went by the presbytery to drop off the letter and from that moment on, I felt free, like a huge burden had been lifted off me. Now I worked only with and for the Lord Jesus and I believed that God would use me if I would do his will.

Two weeks after I left my letter of resignation at the presbytery, Reverend Chavez began pastoring the church in Tarapoto.

My family and I were beginning the great schooling Jesus had prepared for us. If we got good grades, we would then be ready to be the kind of leaders the Lord wants and can use. We headed courageously into the beginning of some major trials.

Discussion Primers

Udelia has left her children behind. Knowing only as much as Narciso has revealed, how does this make you feel? Can you imagine a set of circumstances to justify this decision?

What do you think of the way Narciso handled the adulterous couple in his church? According to the Bible, how should sinful behavior specifically be addressed by Christian brothers and sisters, if at all? How does the above event compare with Narciso's infraction of the rules that resulted in his being sanctioned by the Assemblies of God? Is all sin equal in the eyes of man? In the eyes of God?

Taking on a New Challenge

A small church in the northeast of Peru invited us to come and work with them. I had to travel from Tarapoto which is 30 kilometers into the jungle, to Picota – two hours away by small truck. From there I took a 40-horsepower engine boat on the Huallaga River for about an hour and a half and then I walked for three hours until arriving at the town of Sauce.

This was an enchanting town with a beautiful lake filled with a variety of fish and shells – a remote tourist destination – except for one thing: there were no roads for driving. Everyone got around on horse or on foot.

The first trip I made, Brother Juan Garcia went with me, and my wife stayed at home in Tarapoto caring for our son. I stayed for a week that first time in Sauce, preaching and becoming familiar with the business that Brother Garcia had there – processing yuca. He removed the farina and the tapioca from the plant and exported it to Brazil.

I loved Sauce. There were no mosquitoes and it was a very clean place, only it was so far from our home in Tarapoto. I decided to work for six months in Sauce, preaching in the Northeast Church. The leadership was very strict; the elders dictated the program and even gave me the titles of the sermons that I was to preach. There was some rationale behind this – it was a backlash from having been affiliated with a rather disorganized Pentecostal denomination. They had recently broken those ties and wanted things to be quite different. I tried my best to conform to their expectations.

Every two weeks I would go to visit my wife for several days, then I would return to Sauce. When I came home from Sauce, I always brought with me 70 kilos of freshwater shellfish so my wife could sell them in the market. She gave away to our neighbors what she couldn't sell so they would not go to waste.

Some months went by and I was not content. I had a heart-to-heart talk with some of the leaders of the congregation and told them I simply could not continue this long-distance commute. And so I returned to Tarapoto.

I went to the city of Huallaga to look for work closer to home and my wife and son. I met three families who belonged to an independent Pentecostal church and they invited me to help them. I accepted. They had offered me a place to live with my family but no salary. We had no funds to live on, which was a problem. No money, no food! It's such a desperate situation. While we lived there in Huallaga, my wife not only took care of Gerson, she also taught several young ladies to sew clothing. That brought in some money for food.

I would go with one of the brothers, Brother Marcelino, out to the country to bring back yucca and plantains for our families. We also traveled together to Alto Huallaga to work in road construction. I worked as a topographer's assistant and at night, I'd preach and help out with Bible studies in the church in Alto Huallaga. My construction job ended too soon, though, and it was back to Huallaga.

When I returned I found my wife with arms and legs completely covered with mosquito bites. She cried in anguish and fear, as well. She was afraid of the many spiders that lurked in all corners of that house. Worse yet, one day a group of vineyard workers who worked across the street from us came to our house to advise us they had seen a snake disappear into our house. We ran around like crazy looking for the thing. We found it in the ceiling rafters. The young vineyard workers rounded up the snake and killed it for us.

I found one week of work at home, making earthen bricks. But when I finished the amount for which I had been commissioned, I had to leave home again to find work. One of the ladies in the church, Sister Luz, visited my wife frequently during my absence.

On my next work excursion, I went with Brother Javier to Bombonaje along the Ucayali River in the Amazon jungle. I took with me a significant amount of Biblical literature. We left one Monday morning by truck. After three hours, we arrived at the Huallaga River then took a boat for about an hour. From there we walked, packs on our backs, for 12 hours. We saw nothing but nature – trees, birds and animals – but not the sun; the vegetation was so thick.

On the first day we had no food or water, but we walked until early evening. Just as it was getting dark, we arrived at a small settlement and asked for lodging. Three families that raised cattle lived there. They invited us to dinner which was a fish stew made with small fish and plantains. The fish were whole – intestines and all; they tasted bitter. We were so hungry, so we just closed our eyes and ate the fish. The family put us up on cane beds, but as tired as we were, it didn't much matter. We slept hard until morning.

The next day we continued on our trip. Along the way we found water to drink but no food. We arrived at our work destination just after noon.

The leader of the community welcomed us and gave us a hut to sleep in and food, and in exchange, we harvested beans and corn with them. They gave us a deer skin to use as a bed and a small makeshift kerosene lamp – a can full of kerosene with a wick hanging out the top. The first night, we put our ponchos over us, blew out the lamp and thought we would go to sleep. In two seconds, the room was invaded by a multitude of tiny creatures that were, seconds later, all over our bodies! We lit the lamp to see thousands of cockroaches. Brother Javier and I had to sleep in shifts. With the light on, one would sleep while the other beat cockroaches off with a branch. It was three nights of horror!

The food was not much better. One night they served a hog fat soup – that was the first time I ever ate anything like that.

Nonetheless, for three nights, I preached to the small community in a small chapel. Many of them accepted Jesus and with many others, I left tracts and New Testaments. Now in that community there is a church congregation that serves God. That was wonderful news to me when I learned of it.

As we got ready to go home, we purchased 40 kilos of beans at a very good price and one brother loaned us a horse to carry the load to the river. A young man went with us so he could take the horse back.

On the way, it started to rain very hard — similar to a storm, but without the thunder and lightning. We were completely soaked and we grew tired quickly as the weight of the water added significantly to our load. It was getting late, but thank God, we made it to the river. It was so dark that we couldn't see the road anymore nor would be able to see the boat coming down the river. Brother Javier and I were getting worried. The rain was not letting up and we feared the boat would pass us by in the thick darkness and that we might not be able to hear it for the rain. There was no shelter there to stay the night if we missed that boat.

Suddenly, we heard a motor in the distance. Both of us started shouting and we successfully attracted the attention of the pilot. The boat came to the shore and we got on. It was so full that there wasn't even adequate standing room. We had only inches of free-board as the boat was so weighed down with people and cargo.

Thank God we arrived safely to Picota, a small town of approximately 2,000 inhabitants. We got there at 9:00 p.m. and at that hour began looking for someplace to stay the night. Our problems were threefold: we were soaking wet, couldn't find a place to stay and we had no money to go to a hotel.

We walked several blocks in despair when we saw a woman come out of her home. We approached her and asked if she knew of someplace we could stay the night. She offered her home. There were no beds, not even any furniture, just a tree trunk to sit on. We kindly thanked the woman and went into the bedroom and sat on the tree trunk. It was a hard realization that we would be spending the night in wet clothes sitting on a tree trunk. We were so tired from having walked all day that we soon fell asleep. However, I woke up at about 3:00 a.m. with my body in cramps and could not go back to sleep. I was so happy to see the light of day.

We headed out early to look for a truck headed for Tarapoto. We found one and were headed home by 7:00 a.m. and had arrived by noon. Thank God for his opportune help and care.

My wife, Udelia, had put up a small sign in front of our house, "Sewing Lessons." Our God blessed us by that sign and many young women came to learn to cut material, sew and make clothes from my wife. The revenues from the sewing classes enabled us to eat and buy milk for our baby. Yet the longer we continued to work with the church, helping them to grow and mature, the worse our financial situation became.

≋

My wife and I talked it over, prayed about it and finally decided that we would leave San Martin and travel to Chachapoyas, in the Amazon basin. A picturesque city with a population of 200,000, Chachapoyas sits at the top of a mountain some 2,800 meters above sea level and has many gorges. Socially, it's a very healthy city, though the people are very poor and speak a poorly pronounced Spanish.

There were only two evangelical Christian churches at the time I first traveled there to get familiar with the city and rent an apartment. I stayed a week then went back to Tarapoto to pack for the move and send my wife on ahead of our things, as I had a place for us to live all ready. The truck came that was taking my wife and son, along with a few bags, to Chachapoyas. It was hard to say goodbye to them, knowing they would be traveling alone while I stayed behind to move the larger items. I stayed five days more in Tarapoto before I had everything ready to go, including 2,000 kilos of coconuts to sell once I arrived in Chachapoyas.

As soon as my wife arrived at our new home, she hung a little sign in the window of our new place, "We Make Shirts, Pants and Women's Clothing."

Meanwhile I was traveling with a whole truck full of coconuts to a place called Venceremos, a town between the mountains and jungles of Peru. It rained hard during those days and several landslides blocked the roads. We made it to a restaurant called El Canteño and had to stay the night there.

One night turned into a week of waiting for the roads to be cleared. I started helping out in the restaurant because the owners had told me, "Help us out and we'll feed you for free." Thank God for that blessing. All that week I washed dishes, cut wood, peeled potatoes and more.

Because of the delay and the humidity of the rains, the coconuts rotted and all that effort and cost was wasted. The truck went on back to Tarapoto with the tail gate open, dumping rotten coconuts all the way. There went the capital that we had worked to gather and that we had hoped would sustain us for a while in our new home. Thank God that at least I arrived safely with the rest of our things.

My wife had been very worried because I hadn't come when I was supposed to. Every afternoon she went to the park to wait for me at the time the buses and trucks arrived. She didn't have any money except what we had allotted for feeding the baby and she prayed daily that someone would respond to her sign and commission her to tailor something. She was not able to eat much of anything. She had enough to purchase a piece of bread a day and then she would go to restaurants and ask them to please give her some boiled water to make the baby's formula. Some restaurants would not give her boiled water. She was beginning to feel quite desperate as she waited in tears each day at the park. Finally, one morning I showed up at the house and she was extremely happy and relieved to see me come through the door.

<center>~~~</center>

We started our work at Chacapoyas by distributing tracts at the park, on the streets and in the market. We preached the Word of God in those same places.

We had no money coming in and only a small fund to purchase the baby's formula each day. We would buy a one-liter bottle of milk for Gerson, who was then eight months old, and we'd cut it with water to make it last for almost a week. Our household goods amounted to a bed, a two-burner kerosene cookstove, some pots, pans and kitchen items, a sewing machine and the baby's stroller. We had no other furniture – not even a chair to sit on.

What were we to do? We needed food. My wife and I discussed at length the possibilities of what we could do to bring in some food. I had walked all over the city looking for work in anything in which I had experience – baking, construction, selling goods – and still I found nothing. It was the worst moment for us as a young family. We called on the Lord of our lives, Jesus, as the answer to our problems. Despite our daily difficulties, we kept at our effort of preaching in the open air and handing out literature.

Finally, I decided I would go out into the countryside to look for food. I took some of the plastics we had in the kitchen to trade for food items that wouldn't easily perish. I left on a Wednesday morning very early toward the east. I carried with me a small package of tracts to pass out along the way. I walked seven hours and finally came upon some vegetable fields. In one field was a skinny man with a wide-brimmed hat who was plowing with yoked oxen. I greeted him and stopped for a moment to talk. I said, "I'm a Christian pastor," and I spoke to him about Jesus Christ and the great sacrifice he made for us on the cross of Calvary.

He told me that a professor had once told him that men weren't created by God but by evolution and that the earth had evolved and man had resulted from that process.

I was surprised at the weightiness of his answer and I responded lightheartedly, "Well, professor, if the earth evolved and from it came man, why are not men still popping up from the earth when you till it?" I asked the man there in the field, standing by his yoked oxen with plow in hand if he would accept Jesus as his Savior. He replied that he had accepted Jesus as Savior some years back but he had never met another Christian since and he needed to study the Bible. He invited me to stay the night in his home and said he would invite a group of people for me to present a Bible study. He also asked me to show him more about the Word of God. I accepted the invitation gladly and I sat at the edge of the field and waited for him to finish plowing. He put the oxen to pasture and took the yoke and plow home. We arrived at his house late in the day. I was starving and needed food. We had a dinner of hot vegetable soup with white corn and potatoes in it. As I ate, I remembered my wife and how she and our son needed food, too.

Later we went out to visit the neighbors and invite them to a Bible study that night. Several households gathered to hear the message. I spoke to them of the sacrifice Christ had made to fulfill the Word. After everyone had left, I continued to chat with the family I was staying with about the marvelous Word of God until 3:00 a.m. I showed them scriptures to help them stay firm in faith. They were very excited and continued to ask questions. I gave them some literature I had that they could read and then pass on to their neighbors. We closed the long evening in prayer.

The next morning, I told the family that I had some plastic wares that I wanted to exchange for food that doesn't easily spoil. The brother told me I hadn't needed to offer anything but to just ask because they had plenty for me to take home. I left the plastic wares anyway and they gave me a sack full of 40 kilos of corn, squash, peas, lima beans, green beans, potatoes, carrots, cabbage and more. I was so happy to receive that large quantity of food to be able to take home to my family.

After breakfast, I threw that sack up on my shoulders and started walking. It was 7:00 a.m. when I started and within just a few hours, I was worn out – and the rest of the way was uphill! I had a mountain to climb, no exaggeration! I sat down to rest beside the road, then I went a short way into the woods and found some rope-like vines. I tied the sack with the vines in the middle, brought the ends of the vine around my shoulders, tied it off in a knot at my chest and I started off again.

It was getting late in the day. I had nothing left. I was hungry and thirsty but my heart jumped when I saw the first sight of the city up ahead and I thought, "I'm almost there!" I got home around 4:00 p.m. and my wife ran out to meet me. As she helped to lift the sack off me, we saw that the weight and the vines had brought blood to my shoulders. I was completely exhausted with barely enough strength to walk into the house; but I was happy because that day my wife cooked delicious corn and a vegetable stew. Glory to God!

We continued preaching in the streets and markets and even went house to house. That same week, a box of Bibles for me to sell came in the mail. Brother Julio Valverde, a friend from the Church of Christ in Lima had sent it through the Olano Company. In it was a letter saying that half the shipment was a gift and the other half I should sell at a 30 percent discount to the Church of the Revival.

I went to offer them the Bibles and they would have bought them all, but I sold only part of them to that church and left the money with my wife. I took the rest and went to the smaller towns of Balsas, Celedín, Cajamarca and even Chota to distribute them.

In Balsas, eight brothers invited me to help them in their work, seeing as we were having little success in Chacapoyas. With a great gratitude in my heart, I began pastoring that group.

Ten days later, I returned home to my wife and son and told them about the work in Balsas and we agreed to leave Chacapoyas to work in Marañon, a poor, small town near Balsas.

∿

We packed our things and headed out of town on a small truck loaded with passengers and cargo. The truck left at 4:00 a.m. from Chacapoyas and traveled via a one-lane road that wound around the mountains, hugging drops of some 800 meters to the river below. It was a real problem when we met up with another vehicle. We would have to back up for almost a mile sometimes looking for a spot where both vehicles would fit. It was nerve-wracking to be going around those windy roads with steep drop-offs – in reverse! It was even worse when it got light outside and we could see the massive boulders above us and river far below us.

We arrived at Santo Tomas, a small town in a picturesque valley though very high in the mountains. From Santo Tomas, we continued upward, crossing rivers and climbing more mountains. At 9:00 a.m. we arrived at Leymebamba and we all got out of the truck to have breakfast. Back in the truck, it was higher and higher around more and more curves. We finally reached the tree line – the place above which no trees will grow, called "paramo" in Spanish. It's like a deserted plain filled with thick grasses. We were more than 3,000 meters above sea level in a place called "Calla! Calla!" That means, "Hush! Hush!" and it was probably given that name by traders and salesmen who walked that way or rode on horse or mule back in the late 19th century before the road was built.

The paramo caused two main problems for the travelers of today and yesterday: first, the cold. When you're leaving the jungle, you don't think you will encounter such extreme cold temperatures on the way to more jungle. Many people have died on that mountain range. Secondly, and worst of all, it's a place where thieves hang out and attack travelers. They'll take money, food, clothes, merchandise – anything! That's why it is important to "Hush! Hush!" as you pass through that area. If small children or babies are among the travelers and they begin to cry, the parents will say, "Calla! Calla!"

From there, we headed down the mountains to Marañon. The Marañon River can be seen from the mountain tops. It looks like a huge highway. If a truck were to fall, it would have nothing to stop it until it reached the banks of the Marañon. It was a big thrill for the teenage boys to get up on top of the truck cab and hang on to the luggage bars and look down as the truck was speeding downhill at 30 to 50 kilometers per hour.

As we neared Balsas, we went through a valley filled with fruit: mangos, lemons, oranges, cocoa, coconuts, bananas and even coca leaves. It was a very warm spot – from 35° to 38° Celsius every day – the only season in the valley is summer, all year round.

Finally at 5:00 p.m., we arrived in Balsas. The brothers of the church were waiting there for us. They knew the people who drove the truck and knew what time it would be arriving. Sisters Peta, Carmen, Otilia and Maria were there to meet us, as was Luis Silva. They helped us with our things and Sister Otilia gave us a place to stay for one week.

Balsas is such a small town there isn't much diversity in produce. Only fruit is grown there and in order to purchase other food, one has to travel some 12 hours by foot toward the mountains. Gerson was still not even a year old, and he still took a bottle. In the town of Balsas, there was no place to get cow's milk or if we could purchase it, it was very expensive. So Brother Javier and Sister Maria gave us goat's milk for the baby. I would walk every morning quite early to their house to get the goat's milk for Gerson. It was more than an hour's walk round-trip and it took much time out of each morning.

Discussion Primers

"With the light on, one would sleep while the other beat off cockroaches with a branch. It was three nights of horror! The food was not much better. One night they served a hog fat soup – that was the first time I ever ate anything like that." Narciso and Udelia endure theft of all of their belongings, long and arduous trips (while Udelia's pregnant), horrible mosquitoes, death threats and other hardships. What level of sacrifice would you be willing to make in order to follow your calling? When you're faced with similar obstacles, how can you know whether you are to resist the temptation to give in or whether God is trying to lead you to another path?

The Beginning of the Church in Balsas

We started the church in Balsas with eight brothers. We visited all the homes of the small town and presented the gospel of Jesus to them. Within five months, we had added 25 people to make our regular attendance more than 30 persons. We started with that group to build a house of prayer, eight meters wide by 20 meters long.

We conducted meetings in Balsas, in Coco and Curva, two places that have unusual names for unknown reasons. In Curva, we had services in the home of Brother Alexander and Sister Mercedes and in Coco, in the home of Brother Javier and Sister Maria, all members of the bigger church in Balsas.

My wife and I would walk an hour and 20 minutes, taking with us a kerosene lamp to light the way back at night after the service was over. We would get home at 1:00 a.m. with the baby on my back asleep. God cared for us those nights as we walked through the mountains near the river. The night was so silent as we walked; all we heard was the rushing of the river.

The church grew and became strong. One sister in the church, Petronila, invited me to go to a place call Pacay, on the other side of the mountain. My wife made a lunch for my trip. Petronila put blankets on two donkeys. It's not easy to ride all day on a donkey because they are so uncomfortable, but they are good for carrying things, like the literature and Bibles we had with us.

We left early one morning, stopping only for lunch along the Marañon River. Thirteen hours later, we arrived at the home of a man named Pablo. All day long we had gone up and down hills and mountains. Pablo's family gave us a warm welcome and that night we had a service for the family. The next day we went out to invite the neighbors to come to a meeting in the afternoon. Pablo was our tour guide.

The people in that area have the bad habit of chewing coca leaves – which has a similar effect to snorting cocaine though not near as intense. All the families grow coca for their personal use. That afternoon, many men and women accepted Christ as their Savior and were cleansed by his blood of all their sins. We had combed the area thoroughly preaching the Word. Soon a congregation of 18 people was started. They held services at Brother Segundo Loja's house and he took charge of the new work there.

On another occasion, we traveled even 15 hours more on foot to start a new church in San Jose del Yeso. The new congregations grew quickly and it soon became necessary to visit each of them monthly, taking Bible studies for them and Bibles to the new Christians and tracts for further evangelizing. Each time I arrived, I was warmly received and they were so happy to see me, asking me to stay longer with them. I always traveled with a donkey to carry the literature I had for them, like *The Faith Messenger* from Christian Triumph Company. The work of the Lord grew and became solidly strong. My wife would preach in Balsas in my absence.

Yet Another Ministry

I believe that all true servants of God are ready to assume responsibilities according to the needs that present themselves.

The Health Department had a medical post in Balsas that became available when the local nurse went on vacation and never came back. There was no competent person to take her place or even administer first aid. I spoke to the mayor and asked if he would give me the opportunity to take charge of the clinic and help people as they needed it.

When a woman who had been released from the hospital in Chachapoyas was sent home with some injections that needed to be administered two times daily, the mayor took my offer to help. I was a little nervous when I arrived at the woman's home to administer the shot. Yet she was very grateful because I didn't charge anything. Soon people started coming to my house for me to administer medical treatments, stitch lesions, teach them to give themselves injections and for other simple medical procedures.

Others came with more serious symptoms: headaches, stomach aches, vomiting, diarrhea, lumbago, etc. I would use a medical diagnostic book as I listened to their problems and sometimes I would give them analgesics to ease the pain. Others were sent to me for follow-up treatment or monitoring after being released from the hospital.

As the old saying goes, "En lugar de pan, el mote es bueno," which essentially means that something is better than nothing – the people really appreciated the diagnoses and treatments I provided from my limited knowledge and experience. I became that town's best friend – even the country folk knew me. They were always calling me "Doctor," but I would say, "No, I am just your friend and an evangelical pastor." It was yet another opportunity to talk to people about salvation through Christ Jesus.

There was no way I would exchange my post as minister of the gospel to be a doctor – even if I could have. To me, being a minister is much more than being a doctor. Jesus had called me to serve him through preaching his word, but he wanted me to preach a holistic gospel and I didn't understand that at the time.

The mayor came to me one morning and asked if I could help his secretary. There were a lot of documents that needed to be processed because the outgoing mayor had left things undone and taken his secretary with him. It was a small municipality and I knew the work he needed to have done, so he gave me the keys to the office and when I had free time, I would spend it there processing paperwork.

I was very happy to be able to help the town any way I could and to serve God. The civil register was located in that small city hall and I took advantage of my time there to get the papers of all the church members in order. We had some couples that had been cohabitating for a long time and though they thought of themselves as married, there were no papers. We got them all fixed up in one mass marriage ceremony. I was very happy about that because I felt I could, in good conscience, baptize these families now that their lives were right before God.

The people of Balsas held me in high esteem and respected my family and we gave them our hearts as well, and the church continued to grow.

Exploring New Territory

In fasting and prayer with our main congregation and the smaller ones as well, we soon decided we wanted to reach out to another area, evangelizing with tracts and speaking to people about Jesus. There was a community called Limon nearby and we prayed that God would open the door for us to go there. As always, my wife stayed in Balsas to take care of the church there and I left one morning with a satchel full of tracts and my Bible to walk to Limon, about seven hours away.

The road was rocky and uphill most of the way and it was hot outside – 35° Celsius. I arrived that day at the home of Brother Juan Garcia and we went out together visiting people and inviting them to a service we'd have that night. Later, Juan showed me around his farm, we had dinner and got the house ready to receive people. About 12 people came. One of the best things to come out of that night was that Juan renewed his commitment to the Lord. He had accepted the Lord some years back but was not walking with the Lord. That night he was reconciled and his wife and sons also accepted Jesus.

The way home was much quicker and easier than the way to Limon because it was mostly downhill. I started traveling to Limon once a week to have Bible studies and visit the brothers there. Some 20 people soon formed a congregation and met twice a week.

〜〜〜

We had been praying for the Lord to help us fulfill the great commission to "Go into all the world and preach the gospel." We believed we could fulfill this divine order. Our prayers always included the unsaved in all the nearby towns and communities and our activities always included visitation and evangelism.

Udelia helped greatly with her leadership role in the church in Balsas. That way I could go out to new places to evangelize while she took care of our home church, our home and our baby, as well as being pregnant with our second son, Eliezer.

In September 1982, Brother Luis Silva from the church in Balsas and I had discussed making a trip to the province of Bolivar to take literature and evangelize. It would be the first time an evangelical Christian would bring the gospel to the city of Bolivar or even the province of Bolivar. We left on a Wednesday morning after breakfast and my wife had a meal ready for me to take and eat on the road. I had two packages of tracts. We rode for three hours in a pickup truck from Balsas. Then the road ended. We got off the truck and set out walking the rest of the day — all uphill! At 6:00 p.m., we arrived at the little community of Ingapirca, which has a population of about 500. We approached an older woman and asked her if we would find lodging just out of town in a certain direction. A younger woman interrupted her and said, "Stay here with my family — no one up that road will let you stay with them." So we stayed there with that young lady and her parents. They fed us dinner, and we took advantage of the opportunity to have a Bible study with the family. We talked for about 30 minutes with them about Jesus and then invited them to accept Jesus. The father replied that some time back a group of Adventists had visited their home and he had been thinking about Jesus since that time. Now he was more than willing along with his whole household, a total of six people, to accept Christ. We gave to them New Testaments and some literature to read and study the Word of God. They were so happy and grateful that the gospel had come to their home.

The next morning, we continued our trip. It was a rocky road up into the mountains. We walked for five hours until reaching the peak of the mountain. It had snow on top and it was above the tree line — only grasses grew there and it was extremely cold. Our hands, feet and heads were almost frozen.

With heads heavy with the cold, Luis said, "Pastor, I think I'm going to die in this cold."

In all honesty, it was a dangerous place in which many people had died not only from the cold, but also at the hands of drug traffickers, who often assaulted travelers in that area. We were a little afraid.

It was noon when we began our descent from the white top of the mountain. We were on a very narrow road flanked on both sides with high hills and lots of trees. Luis stopped and said, "Brother Narciso, my father told me that when we get to a lake between these hills, we need to take extra care because it's the most likely place to be attacked on this road."

We stopped and prayed to the Lord for protection and then continued on. We arrived at the lake. (The water is green and the road goes along the shore on one side. This lake is quite a mystery. How could there be a lake so high up in the mountains? What feeds it?) As I looked into the water so close to the edge of the road, my heart began to beat faster. I got an adrenaline rush and my head felt heavy. We started running to get out of that spot and ran for about a kilometer before stopping. As we caught our breath, we saw below us a great expanse with seemingly nothing to break a long fall and above us only sky. If someone were to fall from that spot, the body might never be found.

We were about half-way down the mountain when, to one side of the narrow, rocky road, we saw blood on the ground. It made us both very nervous and I began to sweat. A few meters ahead was a cave just off the road. We had no idea how far into the mountain it went, but we ventured in just a bit and to our terror we saw the head of a woman. There was no body, but we thought it might be further back in the cave.

Brother Luis said in a slow voice, "Brother, look to your left."

I almost fell over! There were the legs of a man along with some other bones. I was horrified! We both took off running as fast as we could with our bags on our shoulders. It wasn't until we almost reached the town that our bodies began to calm down a little.

Still quite nervous, we started to call out when we got close to some houses. We were hungry but didn't feel comfortable going up to a house. We hollered for someone, anyone to come out of their house. A young woman with a dirty face, wearing a large hat and a dress came out and said, "Get out of here! If my father sees you, he'll kill you. We don't give food away here!"

We jumped over a small stone border and started running down the road again and we didn't stop until we got to the city of Bolivar. We arrived there at about 5:00 p.m. and first went looking for somewhere to stay the night, then for something to eat. We couldn't find a hostel or hotel of any sort. Finally, we were referred to a gentleman who took us in and gave us a room with one bed. Eating was also a problem as it apparently was not a custom in the little city to share with strangers. Again, we were blessed to find one willing person, an older woman. She said, "Eat quickly and then leave my house, so my son doesn't find out strangers were here." We did as she asked.

We went from house to house delivering tracts that afternoon until dark, then we rested. And what a blessing that rest was after the physical and emotional trials of that day.

The next day we continued evangelizing using tracts but met with little success. We decided we should cut the trip short and head back for home.

We were going to leave early in the morning, but by mistake, one of us misread the clock and we ended up leaving at 2:00 a.m. – much earlier than we intended. But we were not aware of it for some time. We had planned to leave while still dark, so it didn't seem unusual until some time went by and it was not getting light yet.

At the edge of town we saw a man riding a mule with another one tied following behind. When he saw us from a distance, he disappeared off the road. We started to get scared again, wondering why the man had suddenly left the road like that. We concluded he was probably more afraid of us than we were of him.

The moon was shining brightly and we could see well to walk. As we passed by that dreaded cave again, we were very frightened and it didn't help that the mountain was casting a shadow on the cave so we couldn't see well at just that place. We prayed to the Lord as we passed by there and continued going up the mountain.

We got to the top of the mountain around 6:00 a.m. Again, the cold was almost unbearable. Luis put his hands in his pockets and then down against his legs — he said it was the only warm spot on his body.

We were back in Ingapirca by noon and home later that night. We went to the church to meet the congregation and testify about the mission trip to Bolivar. It had been a very difficult experience for us, although we felt satisfied about having distributed a lot of tracts and spoken to many about Christ.

A Difficult Trial Brings Blessing

Soon after the trip to Bolivar, my wife became ill at seven months pregnant. We had no money and were living on what the Lord was providing through our brothers in Christ. In truth, we ate poorly and were malnourished. Basically, our diet consisted of plantain soup every day. By October of that year, it became evident that Udelia would have to leave Balsas to go to Lima for medical treatment. Our problem was money. The church was poor and only gave us enough to buy the foods that were available locally. However, when I told the congregation that my wife needed to go to the city for medical help, they took up a special offering to purchase her ticket.

In Lima, the doctors examined her and said she had second degree anemia and she needed to eat far more than she had been eating in order to have a healthy baby. It seemed almost impossible in the hardly two months left of the pregnancy to repair the damage that had been done by months of malnutrition. We just didn't have the resources. She went into labor in the last week of November and it was hard for her. The anemia had left her without strength for the work of childbirth. Yet the doctors said they didn't want to do a Cesarean because they feared she would die under the anesthesia.

It was the 28th of November. Udelia was at the hospital in the delivery room and she had nothing left. She fainted. She was transferred to the operating room. It was 10 p.m. and the baby was not coming. The doctors used forceps to get the baby out. He was choking and was purple as he came out of the womb.

Udelia stayed in the operating room for several hours after giving birth. She had lost a lot of blood and needed a transfusion. In one arm they were pumping in blood and in the other arm, serum to nourish her. The next morning at 9:00 a.m., she woke up in the recovery room. What a blessing that the doctors were able to save both baby and mother.

A few days later, they presented her with discharge papers and a hefty bill. She had nothing with which to pay for the blood, the serum, the medicine, and the hospital bed. She knelt beside her bed and started to pray. Jesus was very near to her in that moment and tenderly strengthened her. The glory of God was in that room.

Udelia walked down to the social services office in the hospital to discuss her financial situation with the social worker. The social worker introduced her to the director and explained her situation to him. Then the young lady said, "Why can't we help this woman? We do favors for other people."

The director said, "Okay," and ordered the social worker to adjust Udelia's discharge papers to reflect nothing due. On top of that, they gave her some diapers on her way out of the hospital. Jesus was there that day and he said, "All is paid."

"My God will meet all your needs according to his glorious riches in Christ Jesus," Philippians 4:19.

≈

During Udelia's entire ordeal of infirmity and childbirth, I was in Balsas, about 1,500 kilometers away because we did not have the money for both of us to make the trip. The church and I prayed for my wife's health. We hadn't received any news since she had left on the bus in October.

One afternoon, I was at the port and an employee of the telephone company called me and said, "Pastor Zamora, you have an urgent telegram."

I opened it quickly to read, "Come quickly to Lima. Wife is critical."

I still didn't have any money to purchase a ticket. I ran to ask for help from some of the church members and they didn't have the money either. When word got around, Brother Javier and Sister Maria came to me and said, "Yesterday, we sold a goat. Here, take this money." It was just enough to buy the ticket to Lima.

I spent the night before my trip in prayer asking God to guide me. What should I do? The church had given so much money to us on these two occasions and I felt hugely conflicted about it. I said to myself, "Why can't I have money?" Yet everyone in Balsas was in the same boat – no money. We ate the same food every day – even breakfast, instead of toast, we had fried plantains! Not a person in the town owned a decent pair of shoes – we all wore sandals.

At 7:00 a.m. the next morning, Javier, Maria, Peta, Otilia, Luis and Carmen gathered in the port to send me off. We were praying in the park just before I was to leave when we were interrupted with another telegram. It said, "Don't come. Wife is better." When we read this, we praised God and thanked him. That day brother Javier killed a goat and we had a meal of thanksgiving and sent the other part of the goat meat on to Lima for my wife.

Saying Good-bye

We had congregations in Balsas, Cocabamba, San Jose del Yeso and Limon that I visited each month. We were blessed in Balsas with warm weather, a church under construction and a loving congregation. But when I thought about my wife returning with two babies, I found it impossible to stay there. It seemed there was no future for my family there – no way to make a better life because of the widespread poverty. I prayed for God's guidance to know where he would have us go to start a new mission work.

I went to visit the city of Chota, a medium-sized city with a population of approximately 150,000 and only one evangelical church, a Nazarene church. I felt like that would be a good place to start a new work.

One week later, I returned to Balsas and spoke with the congregation and told them why I felt I needed to leave. Brother Javier Diaz would be in charge and I would come and visit periodically. The congregation agreed on Brother Javier to be the new preacher.

Brother Javier worked in the stone mines for the ceramics factory in Trujillo. I asked him if he would speak to one of the drivers to see if it would be possible to take my bags on one of their trips to

Cajamarca. He worked out all the details and on a Friday in December 1982, I waited, bags packed, for the truck that would take me to my next home.

The Thursday before I left, we had a farewell service, the last one that I would share with my brothers in Balsas. We all cried, from the oldest to the youngest.

On Friday afternoon, the driver arrived and we put my bags on the truck. We stopped in the port and there were Javier, Maria, Otilia, Peta, Luis, Carmen, David and his wife and others waiting. We all held hands, sang a hymn and prayed as more of the townspeople gathered to say their good-byes. After the prayer, we all broke into tears, men and women alike.

The driver started the engine and honked the horn a couple of times indicating he was ready to go. I went up to each of my church brothers and gave each a hug as I cried, telling them the Lord was in charge of this work and encouraging them to remain faithful to the Lord, without fainting. Tears ran down my cheeks like a river flowing. I so loved those brothers and I still do. Even though they were very poor materially, they were rich in the things of God.

I got up on the truck and we left, some of the brothers running behind waving their hands and shouting, "Good-bye, Pastor Zamora." All the way out, the townspeople we passed waved good-bye. The truck went by the long suspended bridge over the Marañon River and I could still see my brothers waving.

I sat crying in the truck and then I started to pray and thank the Lord, asking him to care for the church in Balsas. I cried all the way to Celedin. It felt like I was leaving part of my heart in that town and with that church that I loved so much.

The Work in Chota

I arrived in Chota with a group of brothers from Bambamarca on Christmas Day 1982. I got situated in a small apartment that didn't have electricity or water – not even indoor plumbing!

I was alone all that month while my wife was in Lima recuperating with our newborn son Eliezer and our 16-month-old, Gerson. From Chota, I was able to communicate with my wife and find out when she would be able to travel. It was going to be a hard trip with two babies.

Finally in February, she made the trip by bus. They were to arrive on a Tuesday night. It had rained hard that day that I went to meet my wife and two sons. A new friend, Brother Salazar, went with me and we arrived at the bus station about a half-hour before the bus got there. I was so happy when it pulled up and I saw my wife and sons, especially Gerson, who had grown a lot in the five months we had been separated. He had longer hair and was walking now. It was a very emotional moment for me.

We gathered the bags and headed home. It became immediately apparent with more people in the house that not having a bathroom was a serious problem. We had to walk to the market to use the public toilet during working hours, or out of the city and into the countryside at other times.

We started the work in Chota by evangelizing and visiting families. A church in Bambamarca helped us with an offering when I first arrived in Chota. Then we set up the sewing machine and started sewing clothes. We soon realized that was a saturated market.

We preached in the streets, did Bible studies in homes, handed out tracts from house to house and not one person accepted Christ. We spent several months preaching in the streets and the market and we had no success. I considered going back to Balsas, but when I told

Udelia, she reacted with fear.

"What will I feed my children there? There's no food there and no milk."

We were in a hard place. We continued praying, preaching and waiting for an answer from our Lord Jesus.

One Friday afternoon I received an answer from the Lord God Jehovah, glory and honor to him, when my mother and father arrived in Chota to visit us, which was quite a surprise. They were very happy and had brought with them two horses loaded with 160 kilos of food. I was elated to see them. After we greeted each other, we quickly unloaded the large packs from the horses.

My parents said, "Here are some potatoes, corn and vegetables that we've brought for you." My father added, "We heard you were so close, so we decided to come see you."

That food was sent directly from the Lord to help us stay in Chota. The food lasted us for five months. During that time, we were also blessed with the first people to accept Christ as a result of our work.

<center>~~~</center>

We thought that if the people in the streets didn't want to hear the Word of God, we would preach the message of salvation in the jails. We presented a petition to the head of the federal police detachment and another petition to the mayor asking for permission to preach the gospel of Jesus at 11:00 a.m., Monday through Friday, in the jails. Both the mayor and the police chief accepted the petition and we entered the jail to preach, with Bible in hand, and to pass out tracts.

Preaching in the jails was a formidable experience. The first day that I went in to preach, the officer on duty used his whistle to signal to all the prisoners to leave their cells and go outside to the patio, forming two columns. They had to stand at attention to listen to the message. A couple of months later, when I became better acquainted with both guards and prisoners, I was able to invite those who wanted to hear the Word to come to my sessions and they were able to sit on the bleachers near the soccer field while they listened. Within a short time, 13 people had made a decision for Christ.

In May of that year, one of the prisoners who had accepted Christ got out of jail. I visited him at home and he brought his family to church. They were the first Christians who regularly attended our church meetings.

Later, we decided to add a hospital ministry, going every afternoon to pass out tracts and pray for the sick. On one of these visits we met Brother Artemio Bustamante who was having an operation. We chatted with him, presented the gospel to him and after we explained how to accept salvation, Artemio Bustamante accepted Christ as his Savior.

A week later, he was released from the hospital and my wife and I went to visit him in his home. His wife and his sister also accepted Christ through those home visits and when Brother Artemio was able, he began attending church with his wife and two daughters.

We organized an evangelistic campaign. We made flyers with a make-shift mimeograph made from wood and nylon mesh. We passed out the flyers on the street and invited people to a party for Christ. My wife and I canvassed the city each afternoon inviting people to the meetings.

The meetings went for one week and during that time, God touched the hearts of many people and 25 souls accepted the Lord Jesus. After 10 months of work, God had blessed us with a group of believers.

From there, the work continued to grow. We got a regular radio spot for a program we called "The Eternal Voice." Eventually, the tithes and offerings from the congregation were sufficient to sustain our needs.

The King Circus

In my ministry, I've used a lot of strategies to reach people with the gospel of Christ. One that I'll never forget was a unique collaboration that resulted on the day the circus came to town.

In 1983, the King Circus came to Chota.

One Sunday afternoon on my way home from Sunday school, I went through the Plaza de Armas toward my house and I spotted three brothers selling Christian books and handing out tracts. This interested me and I went up to talk to them. They told me they worked for the King Circus.

The next day, I went to visit the circus and met with the owner Aurelio Diaz and he told me, "I am a Christian, baptized by water, me and my whole family. I accepted Christ in Andahuaylas on one of my trips with the circus."

I invited him to visit me one afternoon.

The next day there was a knock on my door and it was the brothers from the King Circus. My wife invited them to have some coffee.

Brother Aurelio then said, "Pastor, if you would like, we could have an evangelistic service this week, using the circus tents."

I said, "Amen!" and we set the date for the upcoming Friday. That Thursday in the circus performance, they invited the crowd to return the next day for the service and a free performance. The people came on Friday to see the clowns, but that wasn't the main attraction that night – we had the Word of God that transforms lives to share with them as well.

The tent opened to the public just before 7:00 p.m. and it filled quickly. At the beginning of the service, the clowns went out with musical instruments and we all sang praise choruses accompanied by the clowns. After the message, we invited people to accept Christ and four young ladies came down from their seats. They were students preparing to be teachers. That night they accepted Christ as their Lord and Savior.

Later, Brother Aurelio asked me, "Pastor Zamora, would you like to come to Lajas and preach again with the circus?" Lajas was a small community about 30 kilometers away with a population of about 1,500.

I was so happy to be invited. Again, I responded, "Amen, Brother!"

We organized the program for the following Monday and at the circus performance the Sunday night before, they invited everyone to return the next night for a free program. On Monday, I traveled from Chota to Lajas with another brother and we found everything ready at the circus.

The circus tent was already full of people from all around the surrounding area of Lajas.

Upon Brother Aurelio's request, everyone in the circus who knew how to play any instrument participated that night in the singing. I stood in the center ring and we began the service singing praise choruses to the Lord. All the clowns and other circus performers had their instruments and followed along in a big musical jam session for Jesus. It was truly a party for Christ. After singing, we prayed and then I took up my Bible and began to preach a brief sermon entitled "The Universal Flood." After the message I invited the audience to accept Jesus as their Savior, and I asked for those who would like for me to pray for them to raise their hands. Fifteen people did and I asked if they would come forward. From different parts of the audience people came forward to the center where I stood. There they got on their knees and we prayed together as they gave their lives to Jesus and confessed their sins. That night I saw the glory of God in action.

At the end of that service, a tall, thin young man, one of those who had come to the center and prayed for salvation, came up to me and said: "Mr. Preacher, I was a perverse man and almost a murderer. I fought even with my family. Every Sunday when I came to town I would fight anyone I met and every Sunday I would get thrown in jail for public disturbance. Now I belong to Christ. Tonight my mother, father and I all accepted Jesus as our Savior." The young man was very happy that Jesus had come to live in his heart. He went on, "I would like you to come visit my house because I have a very large family and they have to hear the Word of God."

I just stood looking at the young man and finally said, "When would you like for me to come?"

He replied, "Tomorrow."

I said, "Okay, tomorrow morning at 9:00 a.m. I'll be in the plaza next to the police station. I'll see you there."

"I'll bring you a horse to ride because I live way back behind the mountains," he said.

"No, that's okay, I can walk," I replied. "You don't need to bring a horse."

That night I went back to Chota and the next morning, Udelia made me a lunch and then I headed out on foot at 7:00 a.m. to get to Lajas in time to meet Juan, the young man from the circus. I got to Lajas two hours later and found that Juan already had been waiting for an hour.

We walked along the road that goes to the coast for about 30 minutes when Juan finally said, "Pastor, do you see those people on top of that hill over there? That's my home and they are my family."

We left the main road and went up the mountain to his house. When we arrived, there were 15 people waiting to have a Bible study. They all shook my hand. At that very spot, I opened my Bible to John, chapter four. After the lesson, we prayed. The whole experience was new to these people.

The title of the lesson I presented that day was "The Necessity of Salvation for Eternal Life." They listened to the Word of God as they sprawled out on the grass and others sat on rocks or tree trunks. After 30 minutes of presenting the gospel, I invited them to accept Jesus as their savior; 10 of them confessed their sins and accepted the Lord Jesus.

I was elated that in two sermons and two days, God had added 25 people to his church – a true testimony of the wonderful power of God. Jesus does miracles, transforming souls with his power and grace – even those of people who are tired of living.

I spent the rest of that day with the new Christians, answering their questions, and that afternoon I returned home.

The Need for a Church Home

We found a place to use for church meetings in Lajas for the 35 new Christians that had been added in our one month of work there. Brother Alindor Gallardo and his family, the Gonzales family, the Torres family and Brother Joel and Sister Estela had all joined this new work in Lajas. Brother Absalon Torres loaned us his house in which we held services. Eventually, Brother Alindor Gallardo became the preacher for that group and he also went with me to evangelize in new areas and plant new churches.

In July, we had our first baptism in which 20 brothers and sisters were baptized in the Chotano River in Lajas. Many townspeople came out for the baptism. They stood at the shore of the river, others stood on the shoulder of the nearby road while still others sat on rocks and even in trees. When the baptism began, some murmurings were heard among the crowd that we must be near the day of judgment because they had never seen men and women being baptized in a river. All the candidates for baptism were dressed in white and that added to the fright factor for the uninformed crowd. While they spoke of the world coming to an end, we were in the river baptizing our new brothers and sisters in Christ and praising God.

Within a year, the Lajas congregation had grown to have more than 100 in regular attendance. One of the new Christians was a country fellow by the name of Alcibiades Diaz from Olmos.

One day after Sunday school, Brother Alcibiades asked me, "Pastor, will you visit me? I have a lot of family and my brothers-in-law have been going to the Nazarene Church and they need some spiritual help."

I copied down his name and address in my appointment book and that Monday after preaching in the prison, I went in search of that man. I walked for four hours through the countryside. I was getting very tired and looked at my watch and saw it was 6:00 p.m. I tried to ask where I might find the man but no one seemed to know who he was. I decided I would walk half a kilometer more where I could see a house up ahead. I would ask there and if they didn't have any information about Alcibiades, I would have to return to Chota.

When I got to the house, I left the road and approached a man who was tying up some cows. He told me, "Mr. Alcibiades lives in front of those rocks over there," indicating the very direction I had been heading.

In a few minutes I was in front of his house and I called out a greeting. His wife came out and said, "Come in, Brother. Alcibiades will be right back; he went to tend to his animals." They invited me to dinner and then we went to the home of Angelica Gonzales, Alcibiades' mother-in-law. There we had a service and all of the family was invited and attended.

∾

If you can believe it, in that home there were 50 people listening to my message and 30 of them accepted Christ that night – some young, some old. I stayed that night in Angelica's home and the next day left for Chota at 6:00 a.m. so I wouldn't miss my jail ministry. My heart was full of joy thinking of the souls who came to know Christ. Along with my joy, I know there was a party in heaven, as well.

One of the people who accepted Christ that night was Francisco Gonzales. He had been a local bandit, stealing animals and assaulting people to take their food from them. He had been in jail in Chota and from there, he was transferred to Cajamarca to finish his sentence for many counts of assault and theft. The night I met him, Jesus met him too, just where he was and transformed him – making him and his family new creatures. God had his eyes on Francisco to be the leader of that new group. Francisco was truly ready to hear the voice of God and follow it, doing the work the Lord gave to him. He was a great servant of God from then until his death.

Every Monday, I visited the group in Olmos to have a service with them. That church grew each week! In September 1983, we had the first baptism of Christians in Olmos. Shortly after that, a decision was made to build a church. Francisco built it and Sister Angelica donated the property. The congregations of Chota, Lajas and Olmos gathered money for the materials, for the roof in particular. When it was time to dedicate the new building, we had a three-day festival in the great outdoors. We had over 300 people in attendance. We sang hymns accompanied by folk instruments. Without amplification, the preachers had to speak very loudly to be heard throughout the whole crowd. The people of Olmos were astounded. They had never seen a Christian festival, let alone one that lasted three days – it was the first time anything like that had ever taken place in that community.

≈

In January 1984, two men from the church in Chota began attending an Assemblies of God church as well. My feeling is that it had to do with the fact that they were both involved in adultery and I was trying to persuade them that this was not right. Their solution instead was to switch religions.

The two highly influential men had several meetings with regional Assemblies of God leadership and in the end staged a veritable coup. One night after our service was over, the two men, along with some leaders of the Assemblies of God church, arrived at the home where we had been meeting. They announced that from this point on, the church was going to be an Assemblies of God church and they were in charge. The disastrous result was a church divided.

The original, non-denominational effort was left with no more than eight people and we were forced to find another place to meet. Being such a small group, we were strapped economically and we scoured the city looking for a place we could afford. During this time of starting over with the Chota church, the church in Olmos came to our aid and gave us food.

In 1986, we were able to buy a property for the church in Chota. For four years we had moved that church from one rented property to another. We were like a poor old widow without a home. But God is faithful to fulfill his promises. The property we purchased was just two blocks off the central square in Chota – an excellent location. We began a special fund to purchase a church property and received love offerings from all sorts of places. Before long, we were able to realize our dream. That same church in Chota is still alive and well today.

∾

Just after the division of the church in Chota in 1984, we traveled to a small town called Utiyacu with two couples from the church in Olmos who needed to make their civil status formal so they could assume leadership in the church in Olmos. On the trip, we met a Christian couple, the Davilas. They were the lone born-again believers in that community and had no place to attend services. I began to visit them and in just a few weeks, we had added three more couples, all recently converted to Christianity. The group in Utiyacu made four church congregations to which we were ministering. My wife and I realized we needed to prepare leaders for each of those churches.

We made preparations, including drafting a curriculum, and invited eight future leaders to be students in our first leadership seminar – a four-day event. My wife cooked and generally took care of our needs while I gave the classes. The old, makeshift wooden mimeograph served me well in preparing hand-outs on personal evangelism, Christian discipleship, doctrine, basic theology and homiletics. We held another session for the same group later in that year.

The work in that area continued to grow. Upon seeing the need, the leaders in training of the four congregations traveled with me to a new location, Tugusa-Chigrip, to start a new work.

After planting that church, I instituted a regular schedule for visiting each of the churches. On Mondays after preaching in the jail, I would walk for three hours to Olmos for a Bible study. I'd then stay the night there and on Tuesday return to Chota for my morning jail ministry. Tuesday afternoons, I visited the hospital and conducted a Bible study then that night I held services in Chota. Wednesdays after the prison ministry, I traveled to Lajas, visiting families, praying with them and we had the service at night.

Some people who attended the church at Lajas came from pretty far away – with up to one-hour walks to and from church on Wednesday night. Brother Alindor Gallardo from the Lajas congregation hosted me in his home on Wednesday nights. We had an hour walk from church with my brothers and sisters in Christ Rosario Cruz, Anibal, Elisa, Absalon, Absonia and others. With songs and laughter, we would make the long walk pass quickly, arriving to their home around midnight. They had a little room made up for me.

On Fridays, I visited the congregation in Utiyacu – a seven-hour walk. I would get there about 7:00 p.m. on Friday night. It was already dark and I was tired. But as I would approach, the brothers would come out of their houses with their children and sing hymns to welcome me. The Davila family hosted me those nights after the service. I would get up on Saturday at 5:00 a.m. and head home to ready my sermon for the service in Chota. On Sundays, we had Sunday school in the morning in Lajas and then an evening service in Chota. Finally, every other week I managed to get to Tugusa-Chigrip to help the brothers there and encourage them. That trip consisted of two hours in a truck to a little town called Conchan. And from there, a three-hour walk on a stony path, full of obstacles, almost all uphill! It was quite a lot of exercise.

Every congregation was growing in a magnificent way, though I soon began to wear out from the relentless and physically demanding schedule. It was hard on my family, as well. My wife and boys were always in attendance and helping in the congregations in Chota and Lajas. We carried our sons on our backs. Udelia carried the baby Eliezer and I would carry our toddler, Gerson. The church families loved to see my family and to have us in their homes. However, it probably comes as no surprise that after about a year of keeping that schedule, I began to develop heath issues – in my case, kidney problems.

Soon the congregations realized that my schedule was not sustainable. These new creatures in Christ understood that Pastor Zamora could not continue to walk and work at that marathon pace. So together, they gathered a love offering and bought me a donkey to use on my weekly trips to see the congregations.

I felt such joy in my heart knowing I now had a "vehicle" to carry my tracts, Bibles and Christian magazines to evangelize and hand out to the congregations. The donkey was slow, no doubt, but served well to carry my things, including a meal for the trip.

Discussion Primers

"In my ministry, I've used a lot of strategies to reach people with the gospel of Christ. One that I'll never forget was a unique collaboration that resulted on the day the circus came to town." In our culture, blockbuster films, heavy metal rock bands, coffee shops and even bars are some of the "collaborations" Christians have participated in, or perhaps resorted to, to win souls. How far should we take collaboration when trying to reach people for Christ?

Becoming Formally Affiliated

My wife and I discussed the possibility of affiliating ourselves with some mission work in Peru and we visited a few organizations to become familiar with them. The most important standard for us was compatible doctrine. We felt that if we could find an organization that believed as we did, we could be supported in our work and be more effective.

One of the organizations we looked into was La Buena Tierra (The Good Earth) in Pucallpa. I wrote them a letter explaining how I was interested in becoming affiliated with an organization and asked if we could visit. It took them nine months to respond to that letter and it came in the form of a visit from Pastor Nicolas Perez. He arrived very early one morning and said he was there in response to our solicitation.

He said, "I've come to get to know you and be of some help in the Lord's work, if you would like that."

This was my first contact with the Church of God, Anderson, Indiana, with which The Good Earth was affiliated. After that initial visit, we received doctrinal books from them and were visited by another Church of God leader, Pastor Salomon Cabanillas of Lima.

Later, my wife visited the Cabanillas in Lima to learn more of their doctrine and liturgy.

In January 1984, we were invited to a national conference and an inter-American conference. The Church of God welcomed us and we felt good about it — as if it were a natural fit. We stayed several days in the conference activities before returning to Chota.

One of the American sisters who was in attendance at the conference, Evelyn Anderson from Christian Triumph Company, the same organization that had sent us many tracts and *The Faith Messenger*, decided she wanted to travel to our home with us and see the work there.

After the conference, Sister Evelyn, some brothers from Colombia, and my wife and I traveled together to Chepen, where Pastor Nicolas lived, and stayed the night there. That night Pastor Nicolas put together a special service at his church and Sister Evelyn delivered the message. After the service, we said our good-byes to some of the others we traveled with as we were leaving very early the next morning.

After breakfast, we traveled to Chiclayo and then on that same day to Chota – a total of 14 hours on the bus. Sister Evelyn brought with her a gift for us – a typewriter. It was one of the best gifts I've ever received and I was so grateful for that blessing.

Sister Evelyn stayed with us for three days then we all traveled to the airport in Cajamarca so she could catch a flight to Lima. While she was with us, she took many photos and seemed to enjoy herself immensely. She marveled at the bright colors of clothing the young ladies of that zone wear – bright reds and blues. When we got to Cajamarca, we helped her buy her ticket and then had to stay the night because the last flight to Lima for the day had already left. Sister Evelyn stayed the night with my aunt, Marina Zamora, who took her to the airport the next day. I had to start back to Chota that night.

Sister Evelyn became familiar with the situation of the church in Chota and she helped us with an offering to rent a house in which the church could meet and where my wife and I could also live. The church met in that house for a long time, thanks to that offering.

When she returned to Lima, Sister Evelyn told Pastor Bill Taylor of Colorado about our work in Chota and he was moved to leave money with Pastor Salomon designated to buy us a horse, saddle, hat, poncho, rubber boots, a saddlebag and a flashlight to protect me in all weather, day and night, on my way to the various churches.

When my wife traveled with me, she would ride the horse with one child in front of her and the other behind on the saddle. Within just a few months of getting our first vehicle (the donkey), God blessed us with an upgrade to a horse – our new transport to get to the various congregations and small towns.

~~~

In 1984, after my wife traveled to Lima to speak with the leaders of the Church of God in Peru, we realized that it would be possible to work with them since we had studied and decided we agreed with their doctrines. There was also very little difference in the liturgy. We sought affiliation with them through a formal petition to the board of the Church of God in Peru. The organization welcomed us and gladly gave us credentials as ministers.

The churches in Chota and all the surrounding areas we had evangelized – Lajas, Olmos, Tugusa, Utiyaco, Juntas, Balsas, Limon, San Jose del Yeso, Cocabamba and Pucara – all joined the Church of God.

We had to get representatives from all of our congregations together with Pastors Nicolas Perez and Salomon Cabanillas, so we organized a regional convention to orient the leaders of each congregation to the Church of God. We had a good group to work with and all the churches benefited from the orientation. The representatives of each church were as follows: Alindor Gallardo from Lajas, Francisco Gonzales from Olmos, Segundo Davila from Utiyaco, Gonzalo Oblitas from Juntas, Castinaldo Carrasco from Pucara, Brother Mejia from Tugusa, Javier Diaz from Balsas, Brother Maximo from Limon, Segundo Loja from Cocabamba, Jose Eulalio from San Jose de Yeso and Udelia and I represented Chota.

Discussion Primers

Earlier, Narciso's friend Jose asks, "Brother Narciso, is it a problem to work without credentials, free from any earthly institution as long as you're serving Jesus?" What unique challenges are there in freelancing for God? What are the advantages and disadvantages of being affiliated with a single religious organization? Does Narciso's affiliation at this point disrupt his credibility? How do you view affiliations?

Missionary Adventures out of Chota

In 1984, we undertook another adventure, a long and difficult missionary trip, in fact, so distant that my new "vehicle" would be of no use. Brother Javier Vasquez from Olmos was my traveling companion to Querecotillo, where his daughter and grandchildren lived, and from there on to Juntas near Jaen, which is a province that shares a border with Ecuador. My wife helped me pack my old green backpack with 14 kilos, most of which was tracts and New Testaments.

We left from Chota in a truck and traveled three hours to the city of Huambos. We got there at 4:00 p.m. and the sun was already hidden behind the Andes Mountains. At 6:30, I asked Brother Javier, "Where are we going to spend the night?"

He said, "At the last house in this valley, we'll ask for lodging."

One kilometer further down the road, we met a young man who was leading a donkey by a rope and he asked us, "Where are you headed?"

"To Querecotillo," responded Brother Javier.

"And where are you planning on staying the night?" asked the young man.

"At the last house," Brother Javier replied.

"Well, you better turn around and go back to the last house because you already passed it." He continued, "You have to go back about ten blocks and you'll see a large straw house next to the road – that's the last house on this road for quite a while."

It would have been dangerous for us to keep walking that way at that hour. There were a lot of muggers in the area that came out at night. They would take our money, food and anything else we were carrying. The young man said a lot of people had been killed on that road.

Brother Javier didn't seem concerned about what the young man was telling us. He stated again, "We'll stay at the last house further on," and we continued to walk in the same direction.

Later, when it got dark and we still had not found that "last house," I could see Brother Javier was growing concerned. Night was upon us and we were heading down the mountain, struggling in thicket, among trees, rocks and cactus. Brother Javier said, "Pastor Zamora, I think that young man was telling us the truth; there are no more houses and it's true this place is dangerous. I believe everything he said. What would you think if we find a place to sleep behind some of these rocks on the side of the road? Let's sit down behind some large rocks and sleep and we'll get started early in the morning."

It was 8:30 at night. I wasn't so afraid of thieves as I was of snakes, tarantulas and other poisonous critters. I was perturbed with Brother Javier who, I'm convinced, was familiar with that area and probably knew from the start that the boy had been right. I replied, "My brother, seeing as there are no more houses up ahead where we can spend the night, I prefer to keep walking with Jesus who will protect us rather than sleep on rocks."

My bag was heavy on my back and I took it off for a moment to rest. I got out the flashlight and put the batteries in it and Brother Javier got out his flashlight too. We held hands and prayed to Jesus for our protection and then we started out on the road again with our flashlights lighting the way. At times we sang hymns in soft voices and sometime we just talked. We forgot about the danger, and at 1:00 a.m., we reached the bridge that crossed the river that came out of the mountain and ran toward Querecotillo.

When Brother Javier saw the bridge, it was like he was resuscitated; he gave glory to God, and beaming with energy, he said, "Brother, we're out of danger!"

I said, "Amen!"

Just across the river there was a house, so I shouted, "Helloooooo!"

A man inside the house answered, "What do you want?"

I said, "I need a place to sleep. I'm an evangelical pastor traveling to Querecotillo and Juntas to visit a church."

He answered, "I don't give lodging at this hour. A little further on there are some priests and they can help you."

We continued walking through the woods on the rocky path. It was 2:00 a.m. when we came upon another house near the road. It had a light on so we approached, and in front of the house, a man and his son were just arriving on horse from another direction. We greeted them and explained our situation and what we were doing out at that hour. We asked if they would allow us to sleep on the porch of their house. The family was very kind and took us to the kitchen and invited us to a meal – piping hot rice and pea soup. It was delicious and so comforting as we had been hungry on our exhausting walk.

Then they allowed us to sleep on some boards in the yard of their house. They gave us the horses' blankets to put down on top of the boards. I sat down on top of the pallet and fell asleep immediately. At 5:00 a.m., I woke with cramps and pain in my feet from the cold. I woke my traveling companion and said, "I can't take this cold. I have cramps in my feet and legs. Let's start walking so I can warm up."

We left in the direction of Querecotillo, or so we thought. About a kilometer down the road, we realized we were headed in the wrong direction and turned around and retraced our steps. We met a young man who helped us find the right road to take to climb the mountain.

The next place we passed through was called La Raya, a community between the river and the mountains, and then finally we reached Querecotillo at 1:00 p.m. We visited first with Brother Gilberto Gonzales who was very happy to see us. His family invited us to lunch then we rested for less than half an hour and continued our journey to Juntas.

Brother Javier was jubilant at seeing his family at last, and he ran to hug his daughter and grandchildren. After a short visit, we went to see another Gonzales family and others who lived there, including Brother Rodolfo and Sister Carmen who gave me a warm welcome.

That night after dinner we conducted a service of thanks and adoration to the Lord then had a good night's sleep.

The next day we held services from morning until night. Almost everyone in that community was a believer and they all suspended their work to listen to the Word of God. They were a group of Christians without affiliation or formal organization who were each making the independent effort to serve the Lord. During my four-day visit, we established a church structure, and I left them tracts and New Testaments.

Brother Javier stayed in Juntas a couple of weeks visiting with his daughter. On my way back home, I stayed with Brother Gilberto in Querecotillo and held a service that night. Brother Gilberto loaned me a horse to ride back to Huambos, and a young man from the church in Querecotillo traveled with me so he could bring the horse back. I had pains in my legs, blisters and sores on my feet and my toes were bleeding from the almost two-day walk to Quere-cotillo.

That wasn't the last time we went to Querecotillo. I traveled there many times in the years we lived in Chota with other brothers from Chota, as well. We evangelized all throughout that region of the Andes and held many services in the home of Brother Marcelino Gonzales.

In 1985 we traveled from Chota to Juntas again, this time with Brother Jose Tarrillo. When we arrived in Juntas, it started to rain heavily and after two days, the Chotano River had swelled until it covered all the rocky shore. We had to wait two more days after the rain stopped for the river to go back down, but even then we needed help crossing the river.

Brother Gonzales loaned us horses to get us across the river. That was an interesting experience. We entered the river and when the water got so high that the horses couldn't touch bottom anymore, they flipped onto their sides. We, as riders, had to adjust to that by riding astride the sides of their bellies. Then, when they sensed they could touch bottom again, they flipped upright throwing us into the water.

Safely across the river and dripping water, we went on our way on foot and some ten kilometers down the road came upon another river we needed to cross — but this time without the benefit of the horses. We looked it over and decided to try it by tying ropes around our chests to keep Brother Jose and me together. We took our clothes off and put them in our backpacks and held the packs above our heads. When we got well into the river, we realized it was quite deep. We were up to our chests in rushing water. Brother Jose lost his footing and that did it — the strong current swept us both up and took us downstream. Thank God our rope got caught up on some tree branches and allowed us to get control again and get out of the water. If that hadn't happened, we would have drowned. Thank God — he is always caring for us.

When we got out on the other side of the river, we took our clothes out of the backpack and dressed again and started out walking. We arrived at Purcara at 6:00 p.m. and began looking for the home of a Brother Tapia who was supposed to be expecting us that day. He was indeed pleased to see us and invited us to have dinner. Afterwards, we washed up and went to visit some of Brother Tapia's friends and share the gospel with them.

The next day we had an outdoor service of evangelism and 10 people accepted Christ and that was the beginning of a new work in that community. There was one young man among them who was very well versed in the Bible so we asked him to take a leadership role in the new congregation.

One month later, we went back to visit the groups in Juntas and Pucara. On that occasion, one of the new Christians, Sister Oblitas, shared a powerful testimony with us.

Sister Oblitas had left one Thursday morning to take a load of food to her husband who was working in another town nearby. Juntas is high up in the mountains, and it's a dangerous place to live because criminals are always mugging people on the roads leading to and from Juntas. Before she left home, she prayed for God's protection on the way and in crossing the Chotano River. She started out on horseback on the rocky road through the wooded mountains. She sang some hymns in a strong voice on the way. About half an hour into the trip, she came upon three bandits who were hidden behind rocks waiting for a traveler to assault and rob. She was completely unaware of the danger and continued to sing loudly and passed through the ambush completely unharmed without knowing she was in any danger. Later, she found out why.

Some ten kilometers further on, she met a man who was going up the mountain with some packhorses. They recognized each other and greeted each other and continued on their way.

When the man with the pack horses arrived at the ambush spot, the three jumped out to assault him to find that he was the brother-in-law of one of the three bandits. Yet another attempt was spoiled. The bandits asked the man if he had passed the large group of people who were walking with the woman on horseback?

He replied that he had seen the woman on horseback but she was alone.

The men fell silent for a moment wondering who the others had been and where they could have gone. They told the man that she had been surrounded by a large group of people both in front of her and behind her when she passed by their ambush spot. And when they saw all those people, of course, they decided not to jump out and attack.

Some time later, the man met up with Sister Oblitas again and related this account to her. Sister Oblitas believed that she was in the company of a multitude of angels.

"Are not all angels ministering spirits sent to serve those who will inherit salvation?" Hebrews 1:14. God watched out for those Christians in Juntas and many of them had similar stories of God's protection to tell.

〜

In June 1985, we visited Balsas, Cocabamba and San Jose del Yeso with Brother R. Zacarias Bautista. We left from Chota early on a

Monday morning from Cajamarca. We took an old bus that took 10 hours to get us to a community called Santa Lucia where we asked for lodging in the house of a brother from a small, independent church. The next day we traveled to San Juan to get our birth certificates. We took advantage of the time in the city to hand out tracts. From there, we traveled to Celendin, a six-hour bus ride, and then to Balsas by truck for four hours.

The congregation in Balsas was very glad to receive us and we stayed with them for two days holding services and Bible studies. We made a special trip from there to have a service with some relatives of one of the Balsas church members.

Next we continued on foot for 12 hours to Cocobamba, arriving at the home of Segundo Loja. We traveled by way of the shores of the Marañon River. That night we had a praise service and Bible study then rested for our continuing trip. The next day we walked through Cocobamba handing out tracts and evangelizing with Brother Loja while his wife happily made us some food.

Cocobamba is a town situated on top of a very high mountain. The roads around it are sandy and rocky. I don't think it had been evangelized much before. Everyone to whom we spoke and gave tracts seemed very surprised because it was the first time they had heard the Word of God.

That afternoon, we returned to Brother Loja's house for lunch and to get ready for an evening service in San Jose del Yeso, where we had been invited by Brother Eulalio. Brother Loja's wife made us a meal to take on the road.

The next morning, the family saddled up the two horses for us and loaded them with fruit that we were to sell in Santo Tomas. Brother and Sister Loja, a brother and sister-in-law of theirs, Brother Eulalio, Zacarias and I all started out on the trip. We walked along in a group, praying and singing as the two horses carried the load. Brother Zacarias and I often brought up the rear as we climbed to the top of the mountain over a strenuous hike lasting seven hours. At the top, we were above the tree line where only rocks and tall grass grow. It's extremely cold at 3,000 meters above sea level. Fog covered the entire mountain and all the fields.

Some of the brothers spoke up saying, "Let's walk a little faster to get through the Jalca Pass because it's dangerous with both bears and bandits."

We got past that area and came to a water canal. We unloaded our meal, sat down in the grass, prayed and ate lunch before continuing the trip. As we started our descent, the sun started to shine brightly and warm us up. Then around mid-afternoon, Brother Loja said, "Well, Pastor Zamora, we'll see you when you come back through. This is where we part ways since we're going to Santo Tomas to sell our fruit and you're going to San Jose."

It was very pleasant traveling in the company of my Christian brothers that day. We said our good-byes and Brother Zacarias, Eulalio and I headed to San Jose. At 6:00 p.m. we arrived at the home of one of Eulalio's cousins. They were waiting there for us to begin a service. They ate dinner then we began the service. I preached that night and left a package of tracts with the brothers to use in evangelizing. We stayed the night there and the next day continued toward San Jose del Yeso.

In San Jose del Yeso, we conducted Bible studies on Saturday night and Sunday morning. The mayor of the city invited us to lunch on Sunday. We had a wonderful time becoming better acquainted with the city of San Jose del Yeso and its people. It's a very picturesque town on top of a rocky mountain. It has a lot of archeological ruins and we enjoyed walking through the streets sightseeing.

That night we had a special service to wish us well on our trip. The mayor gladly took from us a copy of *The Faith Messenger*. He seemed so happy to have some gospel literature to read and use in evangelism.

After that service, I told the people that if they had any questions, concerns or doubts about any of the things of God, I would like to hear and respond to them. I had no idea that would occupy the rest of the night.

Finally, at midnight, Brother Eulalio said, "Pastor, why don't we end the service now and go get something to eat." So we said good-bye to the congregation and went to dinner — some of them came with us to eat.

I recall looking at my watch and seeing it was 1:30 a.m. Soon after, Brother Zacarias said, "Pastor, I'm not going to walk this trip with you. I'm going to walk one hour to where I can catch a truck to Leymebamba and from there to Balsas. I prefer to walk one hour then ride, versus walking for two days."

I asked Brother Eulalio if I could borrow a horse he had offered to take on the four-hour trip to where his nephew lived. When I finished eating, I sat thinking about how if I left immediately, I would arrive at a good hour in Cocobamba. I talked it over with Brother Eulalio and he then called his son to bring the horse. They saddled it up and at 2:00 a.m., I left on horseback. I said my good-byes to everyone and left my bag with Brother Zacarias for him to take back. I carried only my Bible and some tracts in a small satchel.

I started out on a road that I didn't know went through the wooded mountains with only the light of the moon to light my way. It was bright and I could see fairly well. I started singing hymns to the Lord in a loud voice. I kicked the horse to get it to trot. As I sang, I passed closely by a house and I heard a voice inside shout, "Shut up, you jerk, and let me sleep!"

I kicked the horse a little harder to get us out of there as quickly as possible.

At 6:00 a.m., I left the horse tied to the door of Brother Eulalio's nephew's house and taking my satchel, walked through some corn-fields to get to the main road. At around 11:00 a.m., I emerged from the woods out into the paramo again.

It's like a desert up there where there are no trees. The grasses blow with the strong, cold wind and it's a very lonely landscape with not a person in sight. My clothes were wet from the sweat of walking, and the strong wind soon cooled me off until I was un-comfortably cool. I started running to see if I could generate some warmth. Looking up, I could see a few kilometers ahead where a man was traveling alone. I thought, "If I run, I can catch up to him and we can travel together."

When I got about 100 meters from him, he went down into the water canal but I never saw him come out on the other side. When I got to the canal, I stood on a high rock and looked all around for that man. The canal wasn't that big but there was no sign of him anywhere – no footprints or anything. When I couldn't find a trace of the man, I became afraid. I wondered if he might be a bandit; then hundreds of other thoughts came into my mind at that moment. I tried to force myself to run and within a few minutes, I was at the highest point of the mountain. I stopped and looked back. I saw only fog covering the fields and a light rain began to fall. I started down the mountain to the Marañon River traveling out of the cold.

It was 3:00 p.m. and the sun started beating down on me. Having traveled all night, I was starting to get very sleepy. I was also hungry and thirsty. I found an orange on the side of the road. Half of it was rotten, but half was good. So I threw the rotten half off in the woods and ate the good part, and it gave me some strength to keep on.

At 5:00 p.m., I arrived at Pircas and the home of a Sister Maria. She came out of her house to welcome me and said, "Pastor, if you will rest a moment, I'll make you some soup."

I sat down on a cypress log next to a wall and as soon as I settled with my back against the wall, I was fast asleep. It only took 15 minutes for Sister Maria to get a hearty vegetable stew ready and then she woke me. She was quite a sight. She was perspiring heavily, and her face and head were covered with ashes from having blown on the fire to get it going.

What a delicious stew it was – with corn, lima beans and potatoes! After I ate, I headed out to Brother Loja's house. I was to conduct a service that night. Sister Maria and her daughter came with me.

Brother Loja was waiting for me at the meeting house. It was about an hour until the service began. I greeted everyone then sat on a pew and fell fast asleep and rested for that hour. When the congregation started arriving, they woke me up. I preached that night and dedicated some children and conducted a marriage ceremony! Then we were all invited to the wedding reception after the services.

The reception was held under a big fig tree. There were food, games and songs of praise, and at midnight, they asked me to have a special prayer and a brief message for all the invited guests. The night flew by and I hardly rested at all.

The next day Brother Loja's wife gave me a meal she had made for my return trip to Balsas. The church people had two mules that had been wild in the fields for six months but had recently been corralled and broken for use in transporting people and cargo to and from the port. Two young men, ages 16 and 12, would be my travel companions. After breakfast, we loaded the youngest mule with all the cargo then put a poncho over its head. When I got on, they took the poncho off the mule and it went crazy. It was bucking and running around. I thought to myself, "What a trip this will be." I hadn't had much sleep and was still so tired from the long walk of the days before. The mules were acting up and the young men sent with me were inexperienced.

We made it six hours down the road then came to a gully. The mule that was carrying the boys got spooked and bucked. One of the boys fell to the ground and hurt his foot. He couldn't stand on it and he yelled out in pain when I touched it. I didn't know what to do! I asked the boys to take the mules and go back home and I would continue on foot to the port. They refused, however, and continued on behind me.

We arrived at the Marañon River and got off the mules to have lunch. We unpacked our lunch and ate there on the sandy and rocky shores of the river. After lunch, we got ready to ride the mules again. We got the boy with the injured foot on his mule first, then I put the poncho over the head of the mule I was riding and mounted it. All of a sudden I felt thirsty and remembered that I hadn't had anything to drink with lunch. So I asked the younger boy if he would bring me a cup of water. The boy went to the river to dip a glass of water and just at that moment, my mule got spooked again and kicked its hind legs up and reared up in front. It came down in some thorn bushes right in its face and started to run like mad. From my unstable grip on top the mule, I yelled out, "Mule! Mule! Mule!"

Then I felt that the strap holding the saddle under the mule had come loose. I lifted myself up a bit and the saddle fell out from under me. I wrapped my arms around the mule's neck and wrapped my legs around it, too, as I hollered out in frustration mixed with fear and rage, "Mule! Mule! Mule!" I just kept yelling that.

When the mule finally tired of running around, rearing and kicking, I was still hanging on. The animal settled down and I got off – arms and legs shaking. My whole body felt like gelatin. I couldn't stand. My nerves were unsteady and I was weak – worn out from holding on so tightly. The boys just looked at me in shock!

I rested a bit and then rounded up the saddle and put it back on. I loaded the mule with the cargo again and climbed on its back.

We arrived at Balsas at 6:00 p.m. When I went to unload the cargo from the mule, it reared up at me and tried to kick me as a good riddance, I suppose. We tied it tightly to a tree, so that it couldn't even get its head down to eat, and we left it there that night. The next day, Brother Loja's neighbor arrived in Balsas to take the mules and the boys back. Those mules made me love walking even more.

Brother Zacarias had arrived at Balsas the day before. We stayed one more day in Balsas before returning to Chota. I had gone 27 hours without sleeping and was completely exhausted from the trip. I just needed a place to rest, but I was happy in the service of the Lord.

Another Test from the Lord

My wife became seriously ill. She was two months pregnant and the baby died. The doctors told us she needed to undergo a procedure to remove the fetus and the clotted blood. We had no money and so we had to sell the horse we had been given to ride between missions to pay for the procedure and the treatment she needed afterwards. We thought we might be able to buy the horse back later.

While my wife was in the clinic, I urgently needed money to pay for two injections for her. I left home after I got my boys to sleep and went to ask for a loan from a Christian family from the Nazarene Church that lived near us. The man doubted I could repay him and refused to give me a loan, so I ran to the home of Sister

Rosa Rodriguez and Felicita Tapia.

I just started to tell them what was going on when they broke in and said, "Don't worry, Pastor, we'll buy the injections for you and take you back to the clinic."

I had to run back home to check on my boys. It was 1:00 a.m. when I returned. I entered the bedroom and looked at the bed and it was empty – the boys were gone! I panicked. I tried to figure out what could have happened. I had left the door locked and it was locked when I returned. I started looking around the house and got down on my knees and looked under the bed. There they were, both boys, asleep under the bed. I got them out, gave them some milk, put them back in the bed and, after they fell asleep, I went out again to the clinic to check on my wife. I went back and forth that night from the house to check on the boys and back to the clinic to check on my wife. Thank God, that night my wife started to mend.

Because of the difficult delivery of our second son, Eliezer, and the severely anemic state my wife had been in, doctors had told us that she would need some five years to recuperate between births. Only two and a half years had passed when this pregnancy occurred. Udelia's womb was not able to sustain a pregnancy and we lost our child. We had always intended to have more children but we both realized after this scare that Udelia's health comes first. Reluctantly, Udelia had surgical treatment to prevent future pregnancies.

Though we are full of sorrow to think of the child we lost and others we could not have, we are so thankful to God for the two wonderful boys we have together.

Discussion Primers

"I had gone 27 hours without sleeping and was completely exhausted from the trip. I just needed a place to rest, but I was happy in the service of the Lord." This period in Narciso's life and ministry is very physically demanding and proceeds at a marathon pace. Consequently, Narciso develops kidney problems. Later, the stress in Ecuador and Chile aggravate a stomach ulcer. Can zeal to serve the

Lord at times be damaging to your body? And if so, would God have you "cut back" so you don't "burn out?" Or should you call on God's power to continue at your current pace and overcome physical complications that might be the result of worry and other sin in your life?

Prayer for a New Project

One year at the Inter-American Conference of the Church of God, a major topic of discussion was starting the Church of God in Ecuador. The pastors of Peru and Colombia were charged to enter from the south and north, respectively. Two years had gone by, and no one from either country had taken any initiative to enter Ecuador and fulfill the charge given us in that conference.

My wife and I began to pray and felt in our hearts that we should start the church in Ecuador. In April 1986, I got a passport, which cost $200, and I traveled with Brother Salomon Cabanillas to Guayaquil, the largest city in Ecuador and a major port on the Pacific coast. We knew a couple of Christian brothers who lived there – two young men who had been affiliated with Missionary Alliance and were not attending church anywhere at the time. However, they gave us a cold reception and didn't seem at all ready for the commitment of starting a church. They probably needed to attend a church first.

After two days in Guayaquil, Brother Salomon became discouraged and returned by plane to Lima.

I asked God to help me. As I prayed I resolved, "I have to keep going until I find out where this work should be started." I went on to Quito, the capitol of Ecuador, and from there to Lumbaquí in the Ecuadorian jungle.

I had the address of a lady named Delia Rodriguez. When I arrived in Quito, I went to the home of a Mrs. Paola, Delia Rodriguez's sister. I arrived at 7:00 p.m. and the whole family was making ready to travel to Lumbaquí. They allowed me to join in the trip. That night was torture for me because of the change in altitude.

We went up over the Andes Mountains, and above the tree line my blood pressure seemed to fall. I got a headache, became light-headed, started sweating profusely and had a stomach ache. I could not warm up — it was terrible. When we arrived at Chaco, Mrs. Paola and her family got out to eat at a restaurant, but I couldn't stand and was embarrassed to be in such bad shape.

Mrs. Paola said, "I'd like to buy you dinner; come eat with us."

I just said, "No, thanks," and I stayed in the bus.

As the bus began its descent, I started to feel human again and by the time we arrived in Lumbaquí at 6:00 a.m., I was able to stand again.

I met the Rodriguez family at their farm between Lumbaquí and another town, Francisco Pizarro. I was quite surprised to learn that Delia was not a Christian, yet we had kept correspondence with her for some time.

I took advantage of the time with them and conducted Bible studies for three nights and preached of Jesus. One night before the trip was over, I went with the whole family to the Church of the Covenant in Francisco Pizarro. The leader of the church gave me the opportunity to speak. After the service, I invited the Rodriguez family to accept Jesus.

Delia stood up and said, "I accept Jesus as my Savior, but only if you will allow me to keep going to mass on Sundays."

I told her, "That's no problem. The important thing is that you accept Christ as your Savior with all your heart right now and study the Bible every day. Go to mass on Sunday morning, then on Sunday night, you can come to this church. How's that?"

She promised me she would attend the church two times a week and go to mass on Sunday morning. With those terms, Delia and another family member, Marianita, accepted Jesus as their Savior that night.

We all went back to their farm quite happy, although, Mrs. Paola remained somewhat skeptical. The next day, I needed to leave at midday to go to Lago Agrio to catch the bus back to Quito. I said good-bye to the Rodriguez family. Sister Delia went as far as Lago Agrio with me. She paid for my ticket back to Quito and then treated me to dinner in a restaurant. We walked around getting to know the city while we waited for the time my bus would leave. Sister Delia is a woman with a generous heart. God blessed both her and me through our meeting.

At 6:00 p.m., the bus left the terminal. Upon departing, I made a pact with Sister Delia to send her Bible studies each week and she promised, in return, to study them. I went back to Chota from there to prepare for a regional convention that was to take place in Las Juntas.

Las Juntas Regional Convention

The brothers and sisters from Chota, Lajas and Olmos rented a truck to take us to the regional conference in Las Juntas. Others came on foot. Our truck went only to Querocoto, a nearby town. The brothers from Juntas met us there with three horses to carry our luggage and Gerson and Eliezer, who were the only kids traveling with us. Other mothers had left their children at home because of the difficulty of the trip.

From Querocoto, we walked to Las Juntas, a five-hour journey. The conference took place in August 1986 and lasted three days. It was a big blessing!

There were brothers and sisters there from Pucara and Jaen. The congregation at Las Juntas butchered a cow for the occasion. Brother Nicolas Perez and I conducted most of the sessions while Sister Amanda Itusaca and Brother Jose Luis Chuquiruna headed up the children's activities.

In that warm locale, the children could spend a lot of time playing in the river. Some children were able to catch fish that were trapped between rocks with their bare hands. Gerson and Eliezer were fascinated with the water. However, we didn't take much notice of the mosquitoes that were biting the kids, and that was a grave oversight.

One month later, Gerson fell ill, and we had to take him to the hospital. He was diagnosed with malaria. He was so young and suffered terribly with that awful disease.

Establishing the Church in Ecuador

I corresponded with Sister Delia for three months, sending her Bible studies and encouraging her to remain faithful to the Lord.

One day I received a letter from her in which she wrote, "Pastor Zamora, I would like for us to start the Church of God in Ecuador."

It was a difficult move for me because I didn't know the country nor the Ecuadorian culture, and I didn't have money to rent a place to live and worship. I told these concerns to Delia in my next correspondence and she replied, "I will pay for you to stay at my sister's house in Quito for one month. She'll feed you, and it can be your home base. I know that within a month you will have found a place to stay." This sounded like a good idea, so I discussed it with my wife, and we agreed.

I left Chota in September 1986 and headed to Quito arriving around the dinner hour and knocked on the door of Mrs. Paola's house.

When Mrs. Paola opened the door and saw me she said, "Pastor Zamora, my enemy!" I have no idea if she was joking or she sincerely meant it. Nonetheless, she welcomed me and took me right into the dining room, sitting me at the table where dinner was already in progress. Her husband Lupe was there, as were her children.

Mrs. Paola is a very joyful person. Each night we would open the Bible to read together and pray. Sometimes she didn't want to accept what the Bible said, particularly on the subject of men and women. She would say, "Why doesn't it say 'women,' too?'" She was very sensitive to feminist issues.

On weekdays, she went to work, and I went out looking around the city to see where there were and were not evangelical churches. I went first to HCJB radio station and met some brothers and pastors of Christian churches. They helped me identify neighborhoods that had not been reached. One brother in particular, Antonio, gave me a list of neighborhoods that had no churches and were in dire need of the Good News. And he gave me the address of one person, Brother Angel, who lived in Quinche, one of the under-served neighborhoods.

Next I went to the Bible Society, and they gave me yet another list of places in need of Jesus. High on both lists was a place called Comité del Pueblo. I thought if this place was high on both lists, it might be the will of God to start to evangelize in that area. This was a neighborhood, you might even call it a suburb, north of Quito. I visited there within the week and tried to make some contacts to get to know some people. I did meet an independent group of believers. I started praying for this place every day, and just as Gideon did, I asked God to give me a sign if it was his will for me to begin a work there.

I went back to HCJB and asked Brother Antonio for Brother Angel's physical address. I had written to him and he responded, but now I wanted to meet him in person. One Wednesday morning quite early, after prayer and breakfast, I decided to seek out Brother Angel. I took a taxi-bus to downtown Quito in an area called La Marín and in asking around, found the bus station and boarded a bus to Quinche.

The trees and mountains were beautiful at the outskirts of Quito. We arrived at Quinche and I got off and began looking for the address I had for Brother Angel. I found the house but he wasn't there. His neighbors told me he was a professor and was at present doing research in the jungle. I told them my purpose and they directed me to a group of Christians about five kilometers north of Quinche.

I found the place by asking around and met some of the brothers. They told me they met twice a week but in secret for fear of being discovered by the Catholic Church and being persecuted. The leader invited me to speak that night, and so I stayed, thinking they would also give me lodging. Five more people showed up for the Bible study and I presented a lesson to the group. After we concluded the service, they all said good-bye and went their separate ways to their homes in the country. It was very late and dark, and I didn't know what to do. I walked to the road and waited to see if I could catch a ride with a passing car.

A drunk man sauntered up to me and said, "Hey Mister, no cars will come by here tonight. There's a transportation strike going on in Quito and there aren't any buses either."

I looked at my watch and it was 1:00 a.m. I was cold and, not having much choice, decided to spend the night under the bridge. There I sat with my Bible and satchel full of tracts. At dawn, I could see the road better so I started to walk.

A little while later, one of the sisters from the group I had spoken to the night before, Sister Magdalena, recognized me and said, "Brother, where did you stay last night? Come to my house."

I was so cold I could hardly move my jaw to answer her. I walked to her home and she prepared a warm broth, eggs and coffee. I was so grateful to God for seeing me through the night and now providing this warm breakfast.

A bus heading to Quito passed by at 10:00 a.m., and I was on it. Sleeping under a bridge was a new experience and even though I don't know if it was my sign, in my prayers, I felt led to start the work in Comité del Pueblo.

First, I rented a small room about two by three meters. The owners loaned me two sheets of plywood and a steel drum to put water in. I didn't have a mattress so I just put a sleeping bag on top of the plywood. I was so poor that I could only eat once a day if I wanted to be able to pay rent, too. Some days, I splurged for a piece of bread in the evening. All the money I had was sent by my wonderful wife who, in my absence, was taking care of our children, leading the church in Chota and selling books to support us all while beginning the church in Ecuador.

〜〜
〜〜

One cold afternoon, when the wind was blowing so strong that it was hurling dirt from the road up into the air, I walked to the stop for busses headed downtown, to La Marín. I stood next to a street light with my Bible and tracts in hand, and started singing some hymns – a very familiar one, "There is No God as Great as You." As I sang, some people gathered around me, so I began to present a brief message from Matthew 11:28 entitled, "For Those Who are Tired of Life." At the close of the message, I invited those still listening to accept Christ as their Savior. That afternoon, one lady got down on her knees at that bus stop and confessed her sin and accepted Jesus into her heart. That was so encouraging to me. It seemed to be the sign I was looking for to tell me that I was doing the will of God and that I had the Lord's full support and power. From that moment, I fully trusted God and put myself completely into his hands to be used of him in Ecuador.

The next day, I went to visit the lady and her children and to leave them some Bible lessons.

Next I visited the evangelism department of HCJB, and I rented films to show in the same place I had held my first "service." Three nights in a row, I showed films then preached on that street corner. That week, God saved eight people and a group of kids was always present, as well.

A Jehovah's Witness approached me and offered to rent me a room on that corner. It was three by four meters and had no windows or exterior door. I bought six boards and some bricks and set the boards on top of them to make pews. The Jehovah's Witness loaned me a small table to use as a pulpit. We had our services and Sunday school in that room.

The first ones to come to church there were Brothers Luis and Hugo Silva, and they started to help me with the services. We were joined by the Armas family and then Brother and Sister Agustín and Sandia Ordóñez.

The congregation and I prayed that God would supply us a new place to meet that was bigger. Also, I didn't like being so closely associated with the Jehovah's Witness, particularly because his life was not in order – he and his wife were separated. I felt his presence could be dangerous to the new believers. In my opinion, there was a risk that he might try to influence them with doctrine contrary to what I was preaching and that confusion could split the believers and perhaps even be the undoing of some. God did provide another place to meet that was more central to the neighborhood and closer to the main road. A Sister Lupita's mother rented the second floor of her house to us. There, God blessed greatly by adding new souls to his kingdom almost daily.

In December 1986, I left a responsible sister, Celina, to direct the church while I went back to Peru to bring my wife and sons to

Ecuador. We would live in the same building in which we had church services. The lady rented me a room in her basement, and I even had a bed which Brother Hugo loaned to me.

≈

I surprised my wife with my arrival. I told her how all was going in Ecuador, and we decided she should go back with me. We got everything ready and started out. First we traveled to Lima to get passports for her and our sons. In Peru in those days, one needed the services of a judicial agent to get a passport. I asked Salomon Cabanillas if he would help me with this since we belonged to the same organization. He didn't want to help.

Through another contact, Brother Julio Valverde, I approached the Church of Christ, and they helped me. They even walked me through filling out the forms for the Department of Finance that were needed to get the passports. It cost $100 for each passport, which we afforded from the sale of our things in Chota and with what my wife had been able to save.

I had a letter from the Christians in Action Church in Quito, prepared by Brothers Dale Simpson and Manuel Rea, certifying my work in Ecuador. With that, we presented ourselves to the Ecuadorian consulate in Lima to get visas. They said we would need one more certification, so my wife, with our youngest son, traveled to Quito, acquired the certification and came back to Lima. I say that in one sentence, but the trip from Lima to Quito is quite long – several days by bus, one way.

She had one unforgettable experience on her way to Quito at the Peruvian border town of Tumbes. The bus she was on from Lima had broken down and was running behind schedule and arrived late on a Saturday night at the border. All the offices were closed, and she was not able to purchase an exit stamp she needed to cross over into Ecuador. Nothing would be open on Sunday, so she needed to find a hotel and wait until Monday morning to get an exit stamp. The town of Tumbes was celebrating some festival and all the hotels were full with out-of-town visitors. Udelia walked the entire town looking for a hotel room, with three-year-old Eliezer in her arms.

Many people warned her to be careful because during the festivals, there were many opportunistic thieves. She finally flagged a taxi and asked the driver to take her to the police station. She thought that if there was no place at all to stay in the city, surely the police would allow her to stay in the station. When she arrived at the station and explained her situation to the police, they did not want her to stay the night there.

They said, "We're all men and it wouldn't be proper for you to stay in our barracks." However, they gave her an option. There was one woman in jail and they said she could stay in the cell with her that night. My wife accepted the offer and voluntarily jailed herself for a place to stay that night. She didn't sleep at all that night; she just looked after Eliezer to ensure he was going to get a good night's sleep. She also spoke at length with her cellmate and told her about Jesus. God took care of my wife in jail that night.

The next day, Sunday, she went by bus to a town called Zarumilla and found a place to stay the night, waiting to be able to travel to Ecuador on Monday.

When Udelia and Eliezer got back from Ecuador, Gerson and I met them, and we all went together to get our visas and finalize our paperwork. As we crossed into Ecuador and presented our passports and visas, we had some final difficulties to solve. We had to get a foreigner ID card, and in order to do that, the Ecuadorian intelligence agency of the armed forces had to interview, or rather interrogate, us because we were Peruvians. We took a psychological profile test before a panel of uniformed psychologists and medical doctors.

Even after we were settled in Quito, we were subject to visits by the intelligence officers. One officer came to inspect our home. And another time, when two officers came to check on us, we invited them to have a soda with us and we sat at the table and spoke to them. I opened the Bible and began to witness to the officers. I was surprised to learn that one of the officers was a Jehovah's Witness. We read the Bible and prayed together. Perhaps, because of that crucial day, we were never again bothered by the Ecuadorian intelligence agency.

Lastly, we enrolled Gerson in school. He had to be tested in order to enter mid-year in the first grade. He was six years old at the time. He did well on the exams and was allowed to enter first grade in January 1987. He made good grades and liked his school.

≋

With the official business of moving to a new country concluded and Gerson in school, we were ready to dig into our work.

We spoke to Brother Hugo Silva about our plans, and he told us, "Pastor, I have a place that's a workshop for me right now. I could move my work to the street and the church could operate out of that shop."

We were very happy and grateful for Brother Hugo's decision. We set about putting up sheetrock in the shop, painting and making pews for the new church while Brother Hugo transferred his work to the street. Very few people would inconvenience themselves to do what he did. Brother Hugo commented, "First is God, second is my family and then me." God blessed that brother and within no time, he had purchased another piece of land. That was God's answer.

We started a Sunday school program for children. My wife would get up very early and take water in to clean the "sanctuary." Gerson would sweep and both boys also helped with Sunday school. For the first year, we concentrated on building our Sunday school program.

The place we met was central and located on the main road. It was a good place, but we began to pray for God to provide a piece of property for the church. We had special prayer services dedicated to this purpose and we began a land fund. One night, the unsaved husband of one of our sisters came to church with him. He said, "Put me down for a contribution to the land fund for the end of this month." That sparked enthusiasm.

In 1988, I received a letter from Brother Maurice Caldwell saying he wanted to send me $750 so I could attend the Inter-American Conference in the Dominican Republic. Because of my foreign passport, there was some additional red-tape and I wasn't able to arrange the travel in time. So I asked Brother Maurice if I could use the money he had earmarked for the conference for our land fund instead. Brother Caldwell sent me the check and we prayed that God would use that money according to his will.

We found a property available and went with Brothers Elías Terán and Agustín Ordóñez to find the owner who lived in Tabacundo, about two hours from Quito. When we got there, we asked around until we found him. We met with him and his wife and reached a good agreement. He said he would come one week later to settle the matter and receive payment.

My wife and I went downtown to convert the check Brother Caldwell sent into Sucres (the currency of Ecuador at that time – they now use the U.S. dollar). We put it with the money the church had collected. We then drafted a bill of sale and took care of the other procedures for purchasing property. Then when the owner arrived, we signed the papers in front of a notary, gave him the money and took possession of the property.

The final deed took some six months to arrive, and when it came we went to the owners asking them to finalize the sale, but they backed out and did not want to sign. They increased the sale price of the property. We couldn't turn the property back over to them because we'd already done considerable work on it. We fasted and prayed, asking the Lord to resolve this problem. The owners finally came around and signed the deed.

With the sale of the land complete, we went through the legal process to register the church officially and put the land in the name of the church. The process went quickly and smoothly, thanks in part to an attorney, Mr. Jimenez, who led us through the process. We have always tried to have the legal affairs of the church in order, and God has always blessed us with success.

The Care and Protection of God

While we were busy building the work of the Church of God in Ecuador, our funds were steadily dwindling until there was nothing left.

One afternoon we showed a film in a neighborhood called Pomasqui. Brother Pedro Acosta from HCJB had brought the film and equipment to us. That night after the outdoor cinema and a brief sermon, Brother Pedro approached me and asked, "Do you have financial support coming from Peru or anywhere else? Or do you work somewhere in Quito?"

My reply was: "We live by faith. The Lord helps us to continue this work of starting the Church of God in Ecuador. We don't have any outside support. I can't hold a regular job in Ecuador because I have a missionary visa that prohibits working elsewhere. I can only work for the church."

Brother Pedro took my address and the next day at 3:00 p.m., he and his wife came for a visit. They knocked on the door and shouted, "Does Pastor Zamora live here?" I was upstairs, so I quickly came down while my wife went out to meet them.

In their truck they had brought 50 kilos of rice, sugar, flour, pasta, boxed milk and oatmeal. My wife was particularly surprised at this most generous gift. After they left she said, "Do you think they realize we're Peruvian?"

That blessing was from God who knows no borders or geopolitical boundaries. We thanked God for that food.

One week later, Brother Pedro came to visit again. He said, "Brother Narciso and Sister Udelia, we would like to give you a refrigerator. It's used but if you would like to have it, we will bring it now."

We were elated – we had never owned a refrigerator. We thanked God and left with Brother Pedro to go get the refrigerator in the north of Quito, about an hour away. We went to Brother Pedro's farm, picked up the refrigerator and my wife, children and I were so happy as we headed home with this great gift from God. A refrigerator would have been very difficult for us to ever afford, but the Lord knows our hearts and he supplies our needs. The Lord used Brother and Sister Acosta to help us with food and a refrigerator. God can do amazing things we don't even think to imagine.

≈

I was away on a trip to the south of Ecuador to work with a new group of Bible seminar students. During my absence, there was an attempted robbery at our house. My wife and children were home when three criminals started to come through the window. My wife began to scream and call out for the neighbors, but that did not deter the bandits. I believe they intended to do harm to my wife and children.

One of my sons cried out, "Mommy, I'll go tell Sister Aída to come help us."

My wife quickly responded, "No, son! The bad men are outside and we can't go out there."

Thank God some young people in front of the church heard the screams and came running. The criminals ran off when they saw the group of youth coming to the house.

This was not the worst of my wife's problems. A neighbor to the side of us came on three occasions to the door of the church seeking to attack my wife because we were making too much noise. He complained the noise had shaken some bricks loose from his house and he also railed against us for being Peruvians. Each time he came, I was not there, and he got right up in Udelia's face and threatened to hit her, though he never did.

God has been faithful to protect us. After each incident my wife would only say, "Thank God for all he has done."

Construction Starts on the First Church Building

The new church property had one elevated part so we needed to rent a backhoe to level the land and a bulldozer to clean it. Just at that time, Dr. Firestone and his wife, who were missionaries in Bolivia, passed through Quito. They invited us to have lunch with them in a nice restaurant in Quito. At lunch, he gave us $80 and that money was enough to rent the machinery and get the church property ready for construction. That back hoe removed a lot of dirt from the property. My wife, sons and I all watched with enthusiasm as the big machines left the land clean.

We got the congregation together and started to build the first

Church of God in Quito, Ecuador. Among those in attendance I remember Elías Terán, Jaime Tipán, Agustín Ordóñez, Patricio Heredia, Hugo Silva and Luis Silva. We had pooled our money to buy 2,000 blocks and with cement and block, we built the church. On the days we worked, the sisters of the church would make a large lunch for us while the men mixed the cement and placed the blocks. Eliezer had the best time of any of us, playing in the cement. He was five years old at the time and for days after the construction was complete, he said that he wished we would work with cement again so he could stick his hands and feet in it and pick up the blocks. He loved getting dirty with that work.

A few days later, we held the inauguration of our temple, and it was like a big party. John Stein was a United States Air Force pilot on a tour of duty in Ecuador. John, his wife Rita and their children Jason and Heather had become regular members of our congregation. They brought their video camera to the inauguration and filmed much of it. They also brought guests with them. The church was full of people all celebrating.

How the Zamora Family Lived

How we were able to sustain ourselves financially is another wonderful miracle of the Lord. I often read Habakkuk 2:4, "…the righteous will live by his faith…" and in our first year in Ecuador, we really lived it too. The money we brought from Peru was all spent so we prayed that the Lord would provide a source of income for us, though we had no idea where that might come from or how it might come about. Our small congregation gave us a stipend that paid the rent on our house, but we needed money to buy food.

One Saturday during these hard financial times, my wife went to the market with 500 sucres (which was about $1.50) and bought some vegetables and potatoes. When she got home, she put the food up and turned around saying she was going back to the market. I asked why since she had just been there. She said that on her way home, she found another 500 sucres on the ground and wanted to buy enough food to last us the whole week.

God always provides according to our needs. Our first Christmas in Ecuador, we didn't have any money to buy presents for our children. They wanted a toy car, so we took a shoe box, punched a whole in one side and strung a rope through it. The kids pulled it around the house pretending it was their car. They were appreciative of that simple toy and seemed to understand that we didn't have enough money to buy them any Christmas presents. Udelia was always explaining our situation to them and they accepted it without complaint, thank God. The Lord had many surprises in store for both of my sons, including the ability for each to have his own real car one day.

God blessed my wife and me with some abilities and among them is the skill of sewing. One day we got the idea to make Bible covers. We invested in one meter of vinyl material and we made some Bible covers. I took these to the Bible Society and some Christian bookstores, as well as HCJB radio station and offered them for sale at almost half of what their current supplier from Colombia was getting. Some bookstores asked for a dozen to give them a try. We quickly sewed enough to meet the order. Some, like the store at HCJB, paid us up-front, others, like the Bible Society, paid us after 15 days.

This was the beginning of a blessed work of God. Two weeks later, I went back to all the places that had ordered Bible covers and each of them placed large orders – the covers had sold well. We evangelized, preached and in the down time from those activities, my wife, sons and I made Bible covers. We would work all one day cutting the materials and at night, we would sew. My sons glued the zippers in place and then I sewed them and my wife finished each piece. Soon we had enough funds not only to live on but also to travel to new parts of Ecuador and evangelize.

Discussion Primers

"That blessing was from God who knows no borders or geopolitical boundaries." How is this belief about God reflected in Narciso's ministry? How does it reflect in your own witness and personal ministry?

Narciso raises his children in poverty that, at times, jeopardizes their health. We see his poverty as somewhat voluntary and as part of his life's sacrifice to God, even though he may have lived in the poverty of the developing world had he pursued a secular career. Is it God's will that your children suffer with you in your service to God? Would you raise your children in voluntary poverty for the sake of the Lord? How do Gerson and Eliezer view their circumstances? How do the character-developing benefits of this childhood compare with the stress of growing up in poverty?

Expansion of the Church of God in Ecuador

We prospered so with the Bible covers that my wife and I began to think about buying a piece of land to have our home separate from the church building. Adjacent to the back side of the church were two empty lots and one of them had a for-sale sign on it. One day, I went into town and called the owner to inquire about the price. The price was reasonable, so we made an appointment to meet to close the sale of the property. As it turned out, I knew the owner and we were able to do the paperwork quickly and easily.

However, once filed, it took more than a year for the deed to go through. While we were waiting, we spoke with Brother Manuel Rea who told us that in 1981 the government had confiscated properties belonging to Peruvians. He cautioned us that there might be some problems with having a property in our name.

We didn't know what to do. Should we sell the property or should we list it under the church's name? My wife said, "If God is with us, we won't have any problem continuing to live here, so let's put the property in the name of the church." We listed the Church of God in Ecuador as the property owner.

We purchased the land where the church is now, and the land the church had purchased ended up being the home of a Bible institute and the pastor's office.

～

Our friend and advocate Pastor Mendoza Taylor began to inquire with an American pastor, Sam Harrington, about the possibility of bringing a work camp to Ecuador. Brother Harrington had led several groups to Colombia for work camps. Pastor Harrington and his group agreed to come and a large group arrived to help us build. We had to rent a house for them to stay in. They were going to put a more permanent construction on the church site. We did some preliminary work so that when they arrived they were able to pour the foundation and start building the walls. The plans were similar to a church the group had built in Peru. On the bottom floor there were rooms, a fellowship hall, a kitchen and bathrooms. The second floor was the sanctuary and the third floor would be the pastor's office and the parsonage.

Pastor Sam Harrington, Evangelist Richard Bradley, Maurice Caldwell and Kent Geel organized the groups that constructed the Church of God in Comité del Pueblo, Ecuador. Later, Hugo Silva and I put together plans for the building that is now the seminary. Brother Silva did the electrical work on both buildings and I installed the windows and doors of both the church and seminary building.

Thus the plans we had for building our home on the adjacent lot were transformed to provide not only for a nice place for us to live (on the third floor of the church building) but also a Bible institute that would serve the whole country of Ecuador.

〰

By way of the radio program "Christian Brotherhood Hour," we made contact with many people and one of those was Máximo Cócheres in the town of El Pasaje in the province of El Oro. Brother Máximo worked on the banana plantations.

He wrote me several times, so I sent him literature then finally decided I would go visit him to talk to him about the Lord. I also wanted to see if he would like to work with us. I wrote him about my plans and told him the day and time I would arrive asking him to be waiting for me at the bus station. I told him I would be carrying the magazine La Trompeta (The Gospel Trumpet) so he could recognize me.

I learned later that as Brother Máximo stood waiting at the bus station, he expected to see a tall, fair-skinned man get off the bus. Instead what got off with *The Gospel Trumpet* in hand was a medium-sized man, skinny with dark hair and complexion. I was nothing like he had pictured me! This brought to mind two sayings: "Good perfume comes in small bottles," and "Not all that glitters is gold."

We greeted each other and Brother Máximo took me to his house to meet his wife and to get to know them both better. They were trying to start a work for the Lord there on the coast of Ecuador. This was one good possibility for growth and there were others. Sister Delia Rodriguez had been praying that a work would begin in her town of Lumbaquí. Then I received another letter from a Brother Alejandro from the town of Jima, in the south of Ecuador. He asked for literature, and I sent him tracts and asked if I could visit. Through continued correspondence, we planned a meeting at his house. I traveled from Quito under the assumption that this man was already a Christian and that Jima was a community that was receptive to the gospel. I was wrong.

≈

With my wife in charge of the church and our family, I packed a small handbag of 5,000 tracts and headed off to work in a new area in conjunction with Brother Alejandro. I also had with me three t-shirts to use in evangelism.

I took the bus from Quito to Cuenca, a 12-hour trip. I arrived at 8:00 a.m. and asked around for a bus to Jima. I arrived at Jima at 1:00 p.m. The bus let me off in the central plaza. I heard an HCJB news report coming from a nearby radio and went up to the people listening. I asked them if they had ever met any of the preachers from that radio station. They said they had not. Then I inquired what they would do if they ever met one. One lady replied that she would welcome him and get to know him and listen to him. I handed out some tracts to each of them and went on my way.

I went house by house that day with this hook: I knocked on the door and asked the owners if they would be interested in buying the three t-shirts I had. They were very nice shirts and everyone liked them, but no one could buy them because I was asking too much for them. I didn't want to sell them; I just wanted a pretext for opening conversation with people.

I took the opportunity to ask them if they read the Bible or if they would like to read it. Almost everyone answered "yes," and I left tracts at every house I visited that day. I asked around and finally found Brother Alejandro's grandmother's house; Alejandro actually lived some distance outside of Jima. His grandmother arranged for a young man to take me to Alejandro's house. When I arrived, he wasn't there but his mother and father were.

They welcomed me and invited me to dinner. Later when Alejandro arrived, we had a Bible study. That night he and his mother accepted Christ as their personal Savior. For two days more, we worked handing out tracts, and I left them with a supply of tracts to continue to evangelize in their area.

On the third morning, I woke early to get to Jima in order to catch a bus to Cuenca. When I arrived at the central plaza in Jima, there was a group of women waiting for me. When they saw me, one said, "There he is!" and they all began to walk quickly toward me.

I didn't even have time to say, "Lord, help me!" before they had encircled me – all of them with the tracts in hand that I had given them a few days before. They were enraged and began interrogating me.

"Are you an evangelist?"

I said, "No."

"Then what are you?"

"I'm just a Christian," I replied.

Another woman said, "Are you from the Upper Room Church in Cuenca?"

"That's from the Pentecostals," added another woman.

"No."

"Are you from the Jehovah's Witness Church?"

"Or the Mormons?" another inquired.

"No," I told them. "I'm from the Church of God – the one from heaven above," and I pointed upward.

An elderly woman piped up, "Do you believe in the Virgin Mary?"

"Yes, possibly even more so than you and I obey the commandment of Mary." Then I turned the tables and asked them a question, "What is the first commandment of the Virgin Mary that we should obey?"

They said, "We don't know; what is it?"

I explained, "It says in John chapter two, 'Do all that Jesus tells you,' and I'm obeying Mary because I'm doing all that Jesus tells me to do."

With that they calmed enough to let me through and I quickly got on the bus that was waiting there. As soon as the bus got underway, I stood up and walked around passing out tracts. One person thanked me for the literature.

Despite a somewhat hostile environment, the work began in Jima. One brother opened his living room for prayer services and Bible study. They didn't sing, though, because they feared persecution from their Catholic extremist neighbors. This same brother who opened his home had a fabric store. When I would go to Jima to visit, I'd bring a film and projector and we'd use a large piece of fabric for a screen. He also covered his windows with fabric, too, so we could worship in peace.

God poured out his power and continued to add souls to that secret church. Soon they had a congregation of 28 that met twice weekly. This went on for a year or so. I visited them frequently during that time to help them in their studies. They were happy to be serving Jesus.

When the extremists in the Catholic Church in Jima learned of the solid group, they started a campaign against them. I'm sad to say that the work there was completely destroyed. Some of the congregation left Jima to move to the coast. Of those that stayed, many of them had their houses burned and vandalized, and others had their entire crops burned.

Two years later, Brother Alejandro reinitiated the work there and this time it was no secret. He made it publicly known and his courage was rewarded with success.

~~~

Sister Delia Rodríguez in Lumbaquí continued to ask me to come and begin a work there. I spoke to Brother Máximo about this. His entire family was sold out to God and ready to leave their home on the coast in El Oro and go to the jungle, if needed, to start the church in Lumbaquí. It was God's provision to begin the work in the jungle.

Brother Leonard Snyder from a church in Ohio helped us to buy the church property and the building materials, which had to be purchased in Quito. Brother Máximo built the temple and a parsonage. We were very pleased with Brother Máximo. He dedicated himself to this new ministry in Lumbaquí as well as holding a job to support his family.

The church there began to grow, and we even started an extension service of our Bible institute to train lay leaders and new ministers.

The first trained group from Lumbaquí was: Manuel and Carmen Rea, Delia Rodríguez, Máximo Cócheres and Fernando Chorlango. They studied by correspondence and then came to Quito to be "on campus" for 15 days of testing at the end of their first year of studies. Then we gave them the second-year materials. My wife did all the cooking and also taught Christian discipleship. The other teachers who came for the 15-day, on-campus session were Pastor Francisco Pitty from Panama, Sister Evelyn Anderson from Texas, David and Barbara Miller, missionaries to Bolivia, Pastor Victor Quispe from Bolivia, Professor Israel Osorio and Sister Daisy Taylor and her niece, who came from Colombia. We also had Pastor Nicolás Perez and Marino Guatangare from Peru, as well, and my wife and me.

God greatly blessed us during the years we were in charge of the Bible institute in Ecuador. We graduated some 18 students from the Church of God and other denominations.

~~~

Sister Delia, Brother Fernando and I decided we would like to make a missionary trip just beyond the known tribes that lived on the Aguarico River. On the first day of the trip, we left from Lumbaquí at 6:00 a.m. on foot. On our approach to the jungle we went up and down mountains and made five river crossings. We arrived twelve hours later at a place called El Salvador where there were some small colonies.

We went to the school, began conversing with some of the students and invited them to come to a meeting that night. We left our bags there at the school and headed out to visit the nearby homes and in particular, a family that Sister Delia knew. We took a lantern with us that night by which to conduct the Bible study as the homes had no electricity.

It was the first time any evangelists had visited that place. After we preached the gospel that night, we invited those in attendance to accept Christ as their personal Savior. Four people made a decision for Christ. One of them had a Bible and he stepped up to be the leader to help the others study the word of God on Sundays.

We spent three days working with that group. We stayed with Sister Delia's friends during that time; they fed us, as well. The Lord Jesus is so generous. Though we had a contact in that community, we really didn't know if we would be able to stay there, and if not, where we would sleep and how we would eat (there were no restaurants!). We just knew we needed to preach the name of Jesus and he would supply our needs.

As we were ready to leave, someone gave me a 10-kilo yuca (a tuber vegetable somewhat like a potato) – a big surprise for me! I was very grateful to the Lord and the people of that place.

All the way back out of the jungle, it rained hard. We were completely soaked by the time we got to Lumbaquí at 6:00 p.m. that evening. We washed our faces, even though our clothes were drenched, and got on a bus to take us from Lago Agrio to Quito. The bus left at 10:00 p.m. and we arrived in Quito around 7:00 a.m. Our wet clothes had dried during the trip.

A New Project Proposed at the International Conference

In March 1990, I attended the Inter-American Conference of the Church of God in Guatemala. All of the delegates were in accord to pray for the country of Chile, the only country in South America that did not have a Church of God presence. Pastor Eliseo Aguilar was identified as the ideal person to begin this work in South America's southern-most country.

Back at home, my family and I prayed that the Church of God might go to Chile and in all the countries of the American continents. About a year later, we got word that Pastor Aguilar would not be going to Chile. I talked with my wife about the possibility of us going and whether or not we were ready for a new challenge.

Udelia said, "For me, it's no problem to go where God wants to take us."

We continued to pray and seek the Lord's will. There were seminary graduates in Ecuador who could take over the work we had begun. We spoke to the regional director, Willy Kant. At first, he was not in favor of us leaving our work in Ecuador but said perhaps we could find someone else to take my place in Ecuador.

In 1991, at the World Forum and Conference in Wiesbaden, Germany, a Chilean family, the Riggazzonis, met with other leaders from Latin American reiterating that they would welcome the Church of God in Chile. However, there did not seem to be any pastor ready to meet that challenge.

I also met with the Riggazzonis in Germany, which I was able to attend through gifts to me designated for that purpose. And their plea made a great impression on me. Upon returning home, I spoke again to Udelia and Brother Kant, who then invited a Dr. Patton to discuss the project of bringing in missionaries to take charge of the work in Ecuador. It was our dear friends Nicolas Perez and his wife who came to take our place in Quito. We would leave the seminary under the direction of Fernando Chorlango and Carmen Rea. My wife, children and I would travel to Chile to begin the Church of God there.

We sold a truck we had bought in Ecuador to be able to afford the move. My wife stayed in Ecuador while I went to make some initial contacts and find a suitable place to live. I left Quito in February 1992, and traveled by bus to Chile. The trip took one whole week.

I arrived in Santiago, Chile, on a Wednesday at 6:00 p.m. From there I caught yet another bus to a city on the coast, Valparaíso. Sister Evelyn Anderson had given me the name of a Brother Genaro Fáundez, with whom she had corresponded for some time. Brother Genaro had sent me a map of how to get to his house.

I arrived in Valparaíso at midnight and not knowing what to do, I wandered around a bit. A corporal from the national police approached me and we began to chat. Then he stopped a car and told the driver to take me to the address I was looking for. When I got there, Brother Genaro's wife opened the door and welcomed me. Brother Genaro was not there at the moment.

I was very tired from the long trip and I slept well that night. The next day, the family took me around Valparaíso and that night I participated in the church services that Brother Genaro directed.

The church was Pentecostal and it was my first experience worshiping with that movement. I was quite surprised, if not shocked, as those Chilean brothers and sisters raised their arms up in the air and shouted quite loudly, "Gloria a Dios" (Glory to God). They did it so many times – they must have glorified God a hundred times during that service. I learned that it was their usual custom to shout "Glory to God."

I attended church every night for a week and participated in the services as a member of the congregation. I found it somewhat curious that I wasn't invited to speak; so one night, I decided to wear a tie. I had been going more casually dressed – with a shirt and pants. The night I wore a tie, they invited me to preach. I began to note that the tie was symbolic for them in some way and important. We had a regular Bible study that night, without very much shouting.

On Sunday, after the morning service, the pastor split all the congregation up in groups of two and three and we went walking through certain streets singing and preaching. My partners were two single people, a man and a woman. We walked down one street until it dead-ended into a pine forest. We stood there in front of those pines and began to sing. Then the young man lifted the megaphone to his mouth and began to preach. He was facing the trees and I couldn't figure out why he was preaching to trees – there wasn't anyone around!

I asked the young man, and he laughed as he told me that they always went to the forest to preach because it was known as a spot where depressed people came to kill themselves or drug addicts hung out to get high. We didn't see anyone that day, but I guess there could have been some hidden in the woods.

〰

One morning a Brother Vargas came to visit me, and he told me he had quit the church he was attending because of doctrinal differences. He said he knew of the Church of God doctrine and it was agreeable to him, so he wanted to join with me in starting the work of this church in Chile. It seemed good to me.

I went with him to various parts of the city where he knew an evangelical church would be needed. A bit later, we moved into a room together. It was cheap and for food we looked for restaurants that had a large meal for one price that we could share. The place we lived was plagued with fleas. I bought some flea powder and put it all over the bed and on the floor, but I couldn't kill them. Being bitten by fleas all night kept me awake, and I would walk around all day exhausted. We suffered with those pests for two months.

Brother Vargas took me to a place in the city he said would be the perfect place to start a church, Campodonico, near the beach. This place was popular with young people who came to hang out, do drugs and drink. What better place to start a church? We bought wood for pews, bought a table and with that, we started a church.

I worked in Valparaíso for two months, until April, and then the money I had brought with me started to run out. I called home to Udelia twice and we talked about what I should do. Should I stay and find a way to press on or should I go back to Ecuador before I was completely without funds.

Just at that time, Willy Kant visited me. As regional director and treasurer for the Inter-American Conference, he gave me a round trip ticket from Valparaíso to Cochabamba, Bolivia, so I could attend the conference. The pastors and participants at the conference encouraged me to stay at the effort in Chile and they also elected me as the Conference secretary for a two-year term. In that capacity, in August 1992, I made a trip to Cuba to visit the Church of God there and help them any way I could.

Discussion Primers

In this chapter Narciso once again takes up his sales career. Throughout his life, Narciso supplements his income and provides for his family through sales. How does Narciso's sales career correlate with his missionary status? How can you use your current employment to minister to others and spread the message of God? Or should you even mix work with evangelism?

Throughout the book, there is a stark distinction drawn between Catholics and Evangelical Christians, and nowhere quite as clearly as in the incident in Jima. How do you view the relationship between the two groups? How important and how productive is the distinction between the groups to you? To God? To nonbelievers?

Eight Days in Cuba

For a long time I had felt in my heart that I would like to visit evangelical churches in Cuba, to get to know the struggles in that problematic little Caribbean island. Of course, I never had the money to make the trip. Now, I had gifts specifically for this trip. Jack Wilson sent me $200; William Lamb sent $100; and God blessed with another $300 for that trip. My wife and I started to pray about the trip and decided we should sell our refrigerator that we were so thoroughly using and enjoying. That money along with some other savings would be enough for me to go to Cuba.

I applied for a visa at the Cuban Consulate in Quito. I asked for a visa for religious purposes. They asked me to document what kind of things I would be doing, so I went home and drafted a letter and the next day, when I took it to them, my visa was approved.

The only direct flight from Quito to Cuba was scheduled once a month and the timing was not right. I flew instead to Panama to connect to Cuba from there. On August 30th, I arrived in Panama and visited the Church in Panama City. Sister Martha Burke met me at the airport and her brother took me to and from the airport.

On the 31st, I left for Havana on Cuban Airlines (Cubana de Aviación), which was a unique experience. They called on a loud-speaker for the passengers to approach the plane. Before we got on, a police officer inspected our bags and pockets with a canine patrol. When I stepped into the plane, I saw that the entire business class section had been gutted to look like a big tin can, no seats, carpet or even flooring that you usually see on an airplane. I asked another passenger what he thought happened to the seats and he said jokingly that Fidel had ordered them removed for use in his house.

The views on the flight were beautiful and I could just imagine what Cuba would look like. All the passengers seemed a little nervous about going to Cuba. We arrived in Havana at 3:00 a.m. As I lined up in customs, I prayed for the Lord to blind the customs agents to the New Testaments and tracts I had in my suitcases. I observed that the customs agents wanted to confiscate a package of pasta that the lady in front of me was bringing to her family. While they were fighting over the noodles, I went on to a young customs agent who simply stamped my passport and handed me my bags, letting me pass on through. I thanked God as I left the airport.

Outside, a big, tall taxi driver approached me and asked where he could take me. We rode in his 14-passenger Toyota van to the Church of God in Mariano, Havana. The taxi was very nice; it had air conditioning and a radio. I asked him if the taxi belonged to him and he explained that all the taxis belonged to the government, he just worked for them.

We looked for almost an hour for the church's address and we couldn't find it. Finally, the taxi driver dropped me at an abandoned building that had been a bus station. I paid the bill, $10, and he told me not to worry, that the place was safe, and I didn't need to worry about crime. It was 5:00 a.m.

I entered the structure with my two suitcases in hand and started to approach an elderly, dark-haired, rotund janitor who was pouring water in the toilets to clean them. Then I saw that there were a bunch of people sleeping in the floor of this abandoned building. I figured it must be a place where homeless people slept. As the day dawned and the people started to wake, I handed them tracts and then began preaching about Jesus. This went on for about 45 minutes and a group slowly formed around me. The people were responding to me by saying, "We want this," and "Darn dictator won't give us our freedom." Around 6:00 a.m., a police patrol came by. The janitor came up to me and said, "Hey, friend, quick get in the bathroom!" I darted quickly into the bathroom, leaving my bags sitting there with the janitor. A couple of minutes later, I came out and he said to me, "The cops will throw a person in jail for any little thing and then you don't get out. It's illegal to talk about religion in the streets."

This was God's hand caring for me.

I worked my way to a principal avenue to catch a taxi. It was after 8:00 a.m. and I didn't see any taxis or cars at all. Everyone, men and women, were either on bicycles or walking to their jobs. Finally I saw an old bus full of people coming. Not one car had gone by in the two hours I stood there waiting.

I decided to walk, so I put my satchel over my shoulder and one suitcase in each hand then crossed the street and asked two young men where I might find an evangelical Christian church. They pointed out the way for me and off I went, sweating all the way with my two heavy suitcases filled with literature and some clothes.

I entered into an alley and saw a sign that said, "Salvation Army Home for the Elderly." I thought they might be able to help me there. A young man received me and then called Major Francisco Ramirez.

I introduced myself, handed Major Ramirez some copies of *The Gospel Trumpet*, and asked his help in directing me to the Church of God. Major Ramirez called a Sister Carmen Martinez on the phone and in just a few minutes, Sister Carmen was there, and taking one of my suitcases, she walked me another eight blocks to the church.

It was 11:00 a.m. and I hadn't slept all night. She allowed me to shower and nap; she was a very gracious woman. When her husband, Brother Arturo Fumero, arrived, we spoke of the many obstacles to serving the Lord in Cuba.

They told me there were not many pastors; most had fled the country some time ago. However, people were receptive to the Word of God and they commonly worshiped in houses because it was not legal to congregate outdoors. All the Christian churches in Cuba are very poor in all tangible resources – pastors, Bibles, literature and money.

Nonetheless, the Church of God in Cuba was growing quickly, in home-based units that they call "home churches."

The next day, September 2, I got up, prayed, and took a shower, as was my custom. I was thinking about breakfast as I left my bedroom. I sat down in an old wooden chair and took out my notebook to write. A little later, when Brother Arturo came in, I stood

and said, "I would like for you to come with me to the Panamanian Consulate to get permission to pass back through Panama on
my way home."

While we were talking, Sister Carmen came in and said with
some embarrassment, "Please excuse us, but we don't eat breakfast."

I replied, "That's no problem at all."

We went to take the bus that left some 14 blocks away on the
main thoroughfare. Brother Arturo said there used to be buses that
came closer to his house, but they had been discontinued by the
government.

At the bus stop, one bus went by brimming with people hanging
on even outside the door. It seemed like it would be impossible to
get on that bus and it was the only one scheduled for some time.

Brother Arturo went up to a young woman whose job it was to
supervise the bus stop and explained, "Miss, this man with me is
from Ecuador and he needs to go the Panamanian Consulate." That's
all he said.

I watched as the young woman went out into the middle of the
street and waited there. About five minutes later when a car came
by, she motioned for it to stop. It was a car from the 1950s being
driven by a man on his way to work. All she said was, "Take this man
to the Panamanian Consulate." She didn't say, "Will you please…"
or anything of the sort, just gave him an order to drive us to the
Consulate.

Brother Arturo and I got in the car, and I asked the gentleman if
he worked near the Consulate.

He replied, "I'll take you there."

I said, "Why don't you just drop me near where you work," so he
dropped us off on Cubana de Aviación Street, and we walked to
the Consulate from there.

Most everyone walked in downtown Havana. The people seemed
burdened and had a hungry and thirsty look about them. Even if
they could afford a car, gasoline was very hard to come by.

〰

After I got my papers to return to Panama, we got on a bus and went to the terminal to buy tickets to go to New Gerona Island. We were packed like sardines on that bus. Much to my surprise, a lady near me fainted and slumped to the floor. Some passengers yelled for the driver to stop the bus while others said over and over, "Today for you, tomorrow for me." The bus stopped and a young man took the woman off the bus to take her to the hospital, presumably.

I asked out loud, "What happened to her?"

The passengers around me answered almost in unison, "We are dying of hunger here, sir." Some went on to say, "We don't get to eat breakfast or supper. We only have a little rice at mid-day and that's not enough."

That affected me greatly and tears began to stream down my face. So many of the people I met in Cuba were in fact hungry and de-hydrated. Old men and women cursed the day they were born for having to suffer like they did.

That was Cuba at the end of the 20th century. Downtown Havana was full of dilapidated houses with no paint on the walls. Two or three families lived in every house, and they took turns sitting at the table to eat their one meal a day which consisted of a little bit of rice and some black beans seasoned with water. Most people didn't get supper. Some people drank from hoses because they didn't even have faucets.

Life for Cuban citizens depended on a small paper book. If they lost this little book, they might not get food for three years – which is as good as a death sentence. Each person was rationed a month's supply of food consisting of seven pounds each of rice, sugar and beans, six eggs, half a pound of oil or shortening, a third of a bar of soap for personal hygiene, a cup of detergent for washing clothes, 15 liters of propane gas and, for those who have a car, 30 liters of gas. Electricity and water were also rationed. Children got a bottle of milk a day until they reached the age of seven. There was no toilet paper, instead they used pieces of the sugar carton. And each person got a new outfit only once each year.

This is what everyone got. All of this was purchased in government stores in the area in which the people lived. Their rations were noted in their little books.

Some families didn't make it through the month on these rations and they would have to close down the kitchen until the next rations arrived. The Cuban table never had fruit on it or candies or bread or sodas of any kind.

All the bathrooms were very outdated and many in ill repair. You had to flush the toilet by pouring a bucket of water down it. Showers were a piece of hose hanging from a pipe. Women washed clothes with a substance that came from a native tree.

At the time I visited, the wages for a doctor were $10 a month. One lady doctor commented to me that she didn't even know why they got paid since there was nothing to spend money on. The only stores I saw were stores for tourists — places where they could buy clothes and shoes. But I never saw any grocery store.

Medicine was too expensive for people to realistically afford — except for aspirin, which was what most people used for their ailments. There were good medical services for government workers, but the majority of people could not access them.

The government had some 150 properties, I was told, and they were staffed by maintenance people who worked for food.

Fidel Castro has been a tyrant leader, killing many people. He ordered the execution of his own nephew. Castro's sister reportedly begged for mercy to have her son put in prison for life instead, but to no avail. According to the locals I spoke with, when Castro's mother, Juanita, learned that Castro had his own nephew executed, she had a heart attack and died.

~~~

My hosts took me on a small excursion to an island called Nueva Gerona. We rode first on a bus crammed with about 150 people — all standing because there were no seats — for two hours. The people were all so quiet and no one conversed.

We arrived at the port and had to go through a checkpoint to make sure no one was carrying food out to the island. We got on a boat and I sat next to a doctor. She and I spoke of many things on the way.

A tall, dark sailor with a big mustache got up and announced that we were all invited to have a roll and something to drink. The roll was served on a piece of sugar carton, the same thing they use for toilet paper. The baskets the bread was taken from were dirty and in disrepair. The glasses they served the drinks in were dirty and some chipped. The seats on that boat were also rickety and broken. Hardly anyone on the boat said a word.

The doctor and I talked, however.

I told her, "I saw some people faint in Havana."

She said, "Instead of taking them to the hospital, they should take those people to a good restaurant and feed them a meal. That would revive them."

When we arrived at the island, Pastor Samuel Contino was waiting for us. He took us to his house first, and in the afternoon, to visit the church. He had a program of three days planned for us in conjunction with his Bible institute which, at the time, had 25 students enrolled. In the morning we had conferences on the pastoral calling and its characteristics, and in the afternoon, we visited members of the church. Each night we held an evangelistic service, and the church was full of people – including children who would jump and dance to the rhythm of the choruses.

In our conferences, I was surprised at how Brother Samuel would hand out paper and pencil to each student and at the end of the conference, he would pick up the pencils. It was like they were kindergarten students. It was no laughing matter, though. I felt a need in my heart to help but hardly had any money myself. Nonetheless, I asked Brother Samuel to take me to a store where I could buy notebooks and pencils. He took me to the only place he knew that might sell something like that – a store for tourists. They had only clothes and shoes, nothing to write with or on, I was sorry to see.

The last night I preached on the island, the church was so full of people that there was not even standing room. There were even people standing just outside the doors and windows. That night many were reconciled to God, and six people made a decision to accept Christ as their personal Savior.

I very much enjoyed my visit with both Brother Samuel and his wife, who is also dedicated to the Lord's service.

≈

When Castro first took over Cuba, five congregations of the Church of God were lost. Their locations were: Maquila, Santa Barbara, Camaguey, Cascorro and Matanzas. At the time of my visit in 1992, the Church of God in Cuba consisted of five congregations and some additional smaller house churches. If each of Brother's Samuel's 25 Bible institute students that year had gone on to start their own work, think of the phenomenal growth that could be occurring in the church there. The Cuban Church was helping each Bible student with a stipend of $1.25 a month for food. They needed this money to supplement their regular rations because they were out walking all the time, visiting homes and evangelizing when they weren't in class.

Another brother, Elpidio García, told me he had been taken to jail for handing out tracts in the street. He had written a scripture on small pieces of sugar carton and went to pass them out in Havana. The police spotted him, took him in and it was there that God called him to full-time service. He now has a work with more than 70 brothers in the town of Atanaguildo on New Gerona Island. It is, of course, a house church. And, as is also common with many of the congregations, the people bring a variety of issues – social, political and marital.

If Castro is the oppressor of the people, Jesus Christ is their liberator. Castro says revolution and fight to the death. Jesus says, "I am the life," and, "Whoever believes in me will not perish…"

During that trip to Cuba, I learned even more to love the Lord and his work. With or without money, God's work grows, and great things can be done for the kingdom of Heaven. I continue to pray for the work in Cuba and the pastors there.

Discussion Primers

In Cuba, Narciso encounters a systemic deprivation and desperation that shocks even him. Despite these conditions and no freedom of religion, the church in Cuba is growing and surprisingly vibrant. How is the church in Cuba similar to the early church that faced political persecution? Would you be willing to risk going to jail for your faith? How might your view of God be different if you lived in a society where you could only worship covertly?

The Zamoras Move to Chile

After my trip to Cuba, I returned to Chile. In October of that year, the other directors of the Inter-American Conference came to Santiago, Chile's capital, for a meeting. The Reverends Willy Kant, Victor Ruzak and Lorenzo Mondragón met with me. The group was in agreement, along with the missionary board of the Church of God, to help the Zamora family economically to be able to carry out a Bible Institute two-week internship in November and then move to Chile in December.

That December, the congregation in Ecuador gave us a special send-off. They had a play and some special singing.

We said sad good-byes to all our friends. My wife had many friends and neighbors who weren't members of the church, and many of them cried as they said their good-byes. My sons didn't want to leave their schools and friends there. They looked forward to traveling to a new country, but they wondered how school would be.

We left the work in the able hands of the Silva family.

We sent our things on by boat while we made the trip on land from Quito to Lima and from Lima by plane to Tacna because at that time, the trip by land was dangerous due to the terrorist activities of the Shining Path. At Tacna, we crossed over into Chile and continued on by bus to Santiago.

We arrived in Santiago on December 23, 1992, at 9:00 p.m. A strange city in a foreign country and we didn't know anyone. We soon rented a room in a neighborhood called Santa Raquel – La Florida, on Jacintos Street. We stayed there for five months while we looked for a house.

∼∼∼

The work I started in Valparaíso had faltered in my absence. The person I had left in charge shut down the work, including the open-air services. All the efforts of nine months were lost.

We took advantage of the summer months (December through February in the southern hemisphere) to hit the streets of Santiago and evangelize. We favored the parks. We would rent movies from an organization called Youth for Christ. The director, Eliseo Toro and another couple, Eduardo and Maria Ferrada, were in charge of the projection of the movie. As it was getting dark, we would hand out tracts and tell the people to stick around for a movie. We'd have a small message before the film.

We formed a small group of six people who met in our house. Then some children started coming when we had a vacation Bible school. My wife gave the children snacks each day and made crafts with them and the mothers of the children seemed quite pleased.

Our landlady was an elderly person who had studied the Bible at an institute in her own youth, which was why we were so surprised that when she saw our efforts blooming, she informed us the house was not for holding church services, and we would have to leave.

We still knew very few people in Santiago and we didn't know the city very well, either. We went looking for another place to rent. Our budgeted income was $300 a month, provided by the Inter-American Conference, and we found that the going price for rent was about $200 a month. That would leave us too little to live on.

Summer vacation was ending and we needed to place the kids in school. The Ministry of Education told us our boys would have to test for grade level. Gerson and Eliezer needed stability to be able to study the history and geography of Chile and review all the other subjects on which they would be tested. The entire experience was trying for the boys. I remember Gerson saying through tears, "Why didn't you ask us before you decided to move to Chile? Let's go back to Ecuador."

Eliezer never said a word and tried to do all we asked of him.

Though too late, I finally understood that we must involve our children when we make decisions of this magnitude that will affect them, as well. I still regret that oversight on my part. Now that my sons have grown and are preachers themselves, I think I would like to sit down with them and ask them if they still feel any resentment about not having been consulted on that move.

Despite their anxiety, both boys passed the exams and were allowed to continue in their correct grades in San Pablo Middle School. We continued preaching and daily combing the newspaper for a place to rent, praying that God would guide us to the right place. We saw one ad about a property for sale in Isla de Maipo, Villa de las Mercedes, a town about one hour outside of Santiago. We went to see it and liked it. Of course, summer was just ending and everything was in bloom. We had no idea what winter would be like, nor any idea of how ill-equipped for the cold we were. We bought the property and decided to build on it. From there, we would also plant the church in Chile.

I visited the schools in Isla de Maipo to make sure my sons could transfer. The director said it would be no problem, and they heartily welcomed foreign students.

We did have a problem with getting permission to purchase the land. We needed the right kind of visa. We applied to an organization called Cristo Viene (Christ Is Coming) and they said they would sponsor us if we paid a sum of $150. Then we had other fees associated with our passports along with purchasing the visa which cost $200 each person. Worst of all, the visa would only be good for one year. The following year we would have to repeat the same costly process with Cristo Viene.

Thank God when it was resolved, the Chilean government granted me a permanent visa, the cost for which is only $50! I was able to get this because of my earlier stay in Chile. My family would have to renew their visas after a year and then apply for the permanent visa. I am so grateful for the help of Willy Kant, the Church of God headquarters representative, for his help through that entire process. He advised and aided us in those government transactions.

Not everyone was so helpful. One pastor, Luis Vega, conned us out of $750 promising help with our papers. We went to the police in our county seat, Talagante, and they gave us further instructions on how we could press charges and make him return the money or go to jail. The morning that my wife and I were going to Santiago to pursue the case, we prayed and asked the Lord to do justice in this case. We prayed for God to judge him and we decided not to prosecute. We left the matter to the Lord trusting in His justice.

~~~

On May 5, 1993, we moved out of Santiago to Isla de Maipo. We rented a small house while we put up a hut of sorts on our property in which we could live while we built our house. On the day of our move, it rained heavily and everything — even our mattresses and blankets — got soaked. The landlord of the place we were renting from loaned us a foam pad to sleep on. We didn't have any proper furniture. At first, we got big rocks out of the woods and sat on those and ate on the floor. God had blessed me with tools, so I soon made some furniture. First, just a couple of crude benches, then I bought some more wood and I made bed frames, a table, desk and chairs. My sons sanded down the pieces and my wife helped in all aspects of the work.

Then winter hit. We were unprepared, and my wife was worried how the boys would do in the unbearable cold. My wife and I gathered tree branches for firewood and with a fire we were able to warm up some by the afternoon. We shook with cold every day and my wife was brought to tears.

Right in the middle of this cold season, I had a trip back to Ecuador planned to finish construction on a church building in Otavalo, a town north of Quito. It was the last construction project in which I participated in Ecuador.

When I got back to Chile in August, we started building our house. We put up a wood structure and a place to hold services, too. Soon we had services on our property with the neighbors and their children.

Sister Ann Morgan of Odessa, Texas, sent us money to purchase a piece of property on which to build the first Church of God in Chile. The property was 3,900 square meters, plenty of room for a sanctuary and other buildings.

The next time Brother Kant came to visit to ensure all our paperwork had come through with no problem, he helped us hook the church property to water and electricity.

In August 1994, we became officially registered as the Church of God, a mission of Anderson, Indiana. That same year, we began having regular services in a small location in Villa Las Mercedes.

We contacted Pastor Sam Harrington again about organizing work groups to come build the church in Chile. Sister Ann Morgan and her husband Herb, as well as Doris and Guillermo Barberena from Fort Worth, Texas, came to host vacation Bible school with the children. We held it in two locations, Isla de Maipo and Villa Las Mercedes and had 88 children in attendance between both locations.

In those early years in Chile, we also had visits from Brother Lawrence and a work group that finished the church construction, as well as a Sunday school building.

≋

In 1998, Sister Evelyn Anderson of Christian Triumph Company sent me the correspondence course completion certificates of a Sister Carmen who lived in Nilahue Alto, in the south of Chile. She sent them to me to help in becoming acquainted with people in other parts of Chile and perhaps as a way to expand the work of the church.

I wrote to Sister Carmen about coming to present the certificates to her but I received no reply, so my wife and I discussed it and I decided to go find Sister Carmen.

I traveled from Santiago to Santa Cruz and from there by hired car to Lolol. I got off in the plaza and went to the post office and asked if anyone knew a Sister Carmen in Nilahue. Some ladies there gave me her address – it was about 16 kilometers out of town in the country. I would have had to wait until the afternoon for a bus, but that was a problem because I needed to be coming back in the afternoon. So I decided to walk.

It was 1:00 p.m. when I set out with my briefcase in one hand

and jacket in the other. As I walked down the highway, I started to warm up quickly. A truck was approaching from the rear, so I put my hand out to hail it. I asked the driver if he knew where Nilahue Alto was. He said he knew that he would pass by there but was not exactly sure which little town it was. He said he would give me a ride and he was very patient to help me, stopping at each little gathering of people to ask if we might be in Nilahue. After we had stopped several times, we saw two country men standing near the highway and again stopped. They informed us that we were in Nilahue. I got out and began asking for Sister Carmen. The response I got surprised me.

One of the men I had asked said, "I would like for you to come home with me and have lunch, and then we can go looking for the person you want to find."

I was so hungry that I gladly accepted the invitation. We walked to his house. He quickly heated a meal and we sat at the table, prayed and began eating.

While we ate, he asked me again who it was I was looking for. He thought a moment and then said, "I know her. She's the wife of the one they call 'the pastor.' The name of that good Samaritan is Mario."

After lunch we went to find Sister Carmen. She wasn't at home, but her husband Mario was. I gave him the certificates from the correspondence course and also gave him some Bible materials. I began thinking about heading back to Santiago, but Mario said to me, "Pastor, I would like for you to stay the night here in my house. We can visit a nearby church and my wife should be home soon."

He was insistent that I stay the night. I agreed but needed to call my wife to tell her. We went to find a phone in a restaurant and I called to let Udelia know I wouldn't be coming home that night.

Later that evening, Mario's wife and daughter arrived home. We went to see the church while Sister Carmen made dinner. When we got back, we ate dinner and then studied the Bible together. The next morning before we had breakfast, we had a small service and another Bible study.

Mario said, "The Lord Jesus has visited my house." I stood thinking about what he meant by that and he piped up in further explanation, "I have received the Word of God and I will be blessed."

I went back to Santiago that morning. One month later, I visited Mario and his family again and we went out together evangelizing on the other side of the river. I visited more frequently and Mario became my walking and evangelizing partner. We would leave his house at 5:00 a.m. and walk for an hour and a half, reaching our destination in time to visit with folks in their homes before they went to work. When we called on people, we would pray with them, give them some Biblical literature, have a brief Bible study and then at 10:00 a.m., Mario and I would head back to his house, walking through the woods and crossing the river. Eventually, a group formed in the area we evangelized. Every two weeks, Udelia and I went there to conduct Bible studies. That went on until July 1998.

Discussion Primers

Back in Chota, when Narciso and Udelia have no success for several months, Narciso considers returning to Balsas. Udelia responds to the idea with fear. In this chapter, Gerson and Eliezer react negatively to having to move to Chile without being consulted. Where do a missionary's spouse and family fit into the decision-making process about ministry moves? If Narciso had consulted his sons, they likely would not have been in favor of leaving Ecuador. Scripture urges us to both put family first and yet not let it come between us and following Jesus. What parameters would you propose to live in balance with both of these spiritual mandates?

A Trial that Changed Our Lives

On the way home from a trip to Nilahue, we stopped in Santiago so Udelia could see a doctor about her kidneys; she had been having some difficulties. The doctor informed her that her kidneys were only functioning at 20 percent of their normal capacity and that she would need surgery to insert a fistula very soon. We had no idea her condition was so serious.

One Tuesday morning, Udelia got up to go to the bathroom and when she looked in the mirror, she realized her face was quite swollen. She called me and said, "Look at me." We were both afraid and made an appointment to see a private doctor that afternoon.

The doctor told Udelia that her tonsils were infected. He prescribed some medicine. The next day, Wednesday, she was worse so we went to the community clinic in Isla de Maipo. That doctor said she had bronchitis. On Thursday, she was so swollen that we decided to take her to the emergency room in Talagante. The doctors there prescribed the same treatment as the ones before. We left there with two more prescriptions. On Friday, we had an appointment set at the San Juan Hospital in Santiago with the nephrology department. We were eager to see what they had to say as the prescriptions were not helping Udelia at all.

As we rode the bus to the hospital, Udelia could barely breathe. She couldn't walk once we got off the bus. She put her hand over my shoulder and I tried to support her weight as I hobbled us to the other side of the street. From there we caught a cab to the hospital.

As soon as the doctor laid eyes on her, he ordered a bed made ready and for her to be admitted. I was running around with the papers trying to get Udelia admitted as she sat, almost unable to breathe, in a wheelchair. The swelling had been water retention.

Her kidneys had shut down and water had backed up through her entire body.

A paramedic wheeled Udelia to the third floor, the nephrology department. At the door of the examination room, we said good-bye. Udelia said, "If something happens and I am not able to go home, take care of my Eliezer. That boy needs care and help – don't leave him."

I went home carrying my wife's clothes and purse. It didn't seem real that she could be in the hospital. I was so sad as I entered the house. When the boys got home from school, I had to prepare their meal. I walked into the kitchen and thought to myself, "What should I make?" I cried because of how helpless I was even to cook a meal. That first meal I made was an unsavory, bland soup. My sons ate it so as not to discourage me, though they commented that they wished their mother was there to tell us how to make the soup.

The next day, I went back to the hospital and took some of Udelia's things. The doctors had been trying to drain the water from her body by giving her intravenous furosemide, a potent diuretic. This just seemed to make her worse. To add to this misery, she was not allowed to eat anything except greens with no salt.

While my wife suffered in the hospital, at home we had to completely reorganize the division of labor and our work in the church and home office. Gerson and Eliezer spent all Saturday doing the laundry and cleaning the house. They each ironed their school uniforms and in the mornings, they made their own breakfast now that their mother was not there to do it for them.

These first days were difficult – especially learning to cook. Gerson and Eliezer cried because they missed and worried about their mother. We all went to church on Sunday, and on Monday, the boys started back to school and I headed back to the hospital.

Udelia had been in the hospital for a week and they still had not successfully dealt with her water retention. A team of three doctors discussed my wife's case. Their prognosis: "Udelia has a terminal chronic kidney failure."

On Thursday, when I arrived at the hospital the doctors told me that as Udelia's husband, I would have to authorize her treatment.

The medical team had decided to place a catheter in her neck and from there to perform dialysis on her.

I replied, "I can't allow you to put a catheter in her neck. Please, place a fistula in her arm. God has taken care of her up to this point and he will continue to do so." I refused to authorize the catheter. The medical team said I had one day to move my wife from the hospital.

When I got to the hospital on Friday, I was surprised to see that Udelia was not even able to sit upright. The nurses in the room with us said to me, "Sir, your wife fainted several times last night. The doctors and nurses have had to be very attentive to her throughout the night. Your wife's condition is critical."

As I was listening to the nurses, the medical team came in and one said to me, "You must accept the catheter."

I looked at my wife who was unable to talk or even move and I said, "She is your patient, doctor, if that is what's best for her health, very well then."

That night they put the catheter in and on Saturday, they transferred her to the hospital in Talagante. This was so much more convenient because it was more than an hour each way to travel to Santiago, whereas the hospital at Talagante was only 15 minutes from our home. Now our sons could visit their mother more frequently, and they did.

Early that Saturday morning, I went in to Santiago to help with the transfer to Talagante. From the hospital in Santiago, I called the Horizon Dialysis Center and they reserved a machine for her immediately. We waited there in Santiago for the ambulance to arrive to take Udelia to Talagante. The entire morning went by and still no ambulance. I got desperate and called a friend, Brother Guillermo Arias. He came with his truck and we were going to take her to Talagante ourselves, but the hospital attendants would not allow it. They said since she was going from one medical facility to another, she had to be transported by ambulance.

Finally at 2:00 p.m. the ambulance arrived, thank God. They put Udelia in and I was able to ride with her to comfort and care for her on the trip. The ambulance took her directly to the dialysis center and they were able to fit her in. That night when her dialysis was complete, I took her in a truck to the Talagante hospital. I tucked her in bed and headed back to the house.

The next day, Sunday, the whole family was together in Udelia's hospital room. My sons were elated to see their mother again after a week.

For a short while then, we had a new routine. After getting the boys off to school, I would go pick Udelia up from the hospital and take her to the dialysis center. She would finish dialysis around noon, and then I would take her back to the hospital and hurry home to fix the boys their lunch, do other chores and some work at home. After Gerson and Eliezer finished school in the afternoon, they would go for a short while to visit their mother.

After about a week, Udelia was given permission to go home. Then our schedule changed again. Our days began with a dialysis van picking Udelia up at 6:00 a.m. to take her to the Center. She would begin dialysis at 7:30 a.m.

The machine cleansed her blood of all the toxins and water, among other things, that the kidneys usually get out of our system. However necessary, dialysis is hard on the body. The heart has to work extra during dialysis and many people who regularly take dialysis end up dying of heart failure, as I understand.

Udelia cried each morning as it was time for her to go to dialysis. She prayed, "Lord, help me be able to bear the pain. Don't take my pain from me, but help me to bear it." She said the worst part of the process for her was when they inserted the dialysis needles in her skin.

My sons and I sympathized with Udelia's physical torture. Her suffering caused us great emotional pain.

Finally one day, brimming over with the stress of it all, Gerson broke down and in sobs said to his mother, "Mama, why is God doing this to you? You have served him, so why is this happening to you? I can't believe it."

Udelia gathered her strength and replied, "Son, this is just a trial and it's one of the ways I know that God loves me. The devil wants me to blaspheme the name of God, but we have the victory in

Jesus."

However, Gerson's words worried my wife and she asked me later, "Please, pray for Gerson that he doesn't resent the Lord Jesus. This is very dangerous because he seems to be blaming God. We have to encourage him to remain faithful to the Lord – he's a young man now."

〜〜〜

One day while my wife was in dialysis, I met with the directors of the Center to discuss the costs and what to expect in the future. They explained to me how to apply for federal insurance benefits for her and how those benefits would pay for the dialysis. They said she would be eligible for disability benefits. They also told me that a person on dialysis can only expect to live about five years.

I did all the paperwork and in 1999, we received her federal insurance card which would pay for one half of the dialysis cost. The other half was paid by a National Health Fund loan.

The doctor at the dialysis center encouraged Udelia to undergo the necessary procedures to prepare for a kidney transplant. This gave us some hope and so we went to the San Juan Hospital in Santiago and began the procedures. Many of them were painful for Udelia but she seemed expectant and strong. She continued praying to the Lord as she underwent all the procedures.

On December 20, 1999, Udelia registered at the National Health Center and was put on the waiting list for a new kidney. Meanwhile, she continued with dialysis. At this same time, we were ministering to a group of drug-addicted women. My wife was able to forget about her own troubles as she ministered to those women whose lives and bodies had been ruined by drugs.

〜〜〜

Though it is not even in the same league as Udelia's suffering, the boys and I suffered, as well. It did not take us long to realize how valuable she had been in the home. All the work she did now fell on us and the majority of it on me. And more times than I care to remember, the van did not show up to take her to dialysis, so I dropped everything and rushed her there, stayed with her until they hooked her up, rushed back home to get as much done as I could, then back to the Center to pick her up.

All the projects I had in process came to a screeching halt when Udelia took ill. My new projects were cooking, taking care of my wife and sons, and doing the minimum needed to maintain the pastoral responsibilities of the church in Isla de Maipo. The excessive work and worry irritated an old ulcer I had developed long ago. I became depressed.

For days I felt like I didn't want to go on like this. I couldn't wait until night came and I wished I would just disappear into the darkness, off the face of the earth. Against my very will, and mostly out of habit I guess, I got down on my knees to pray and read the Bible. Sometimes I just couldn't do it, because I was so focused on my problems and not focused on Jesus.

I found my medicine in Philippians 4:6-20, "Do not be anxious about anything, but in everything, by prayer and petition, with thanksgiving, present your requests to God..." And Matthew 6: "Therefore I tell you, do not worry about your life, what you will eat or drink; or about your body, what you will wear. Is not life more important than food, and the body more important than clothes? ... Who of you by worrying can add a single hour to his life?"

Discussion Primers

As Udelia falls ill and he has to take her place, Narciso realizes the work she has done over the years. Compare, contrast and discuss the relationship of Udelia's service and ministry to that of Narciso's.

Battles for Christ

In my last year of seminary, my class was in charge of putting together our yearbook. Each of the seniors had to provide a picture and for the opposite side of the page, a Bible verse. The verse that captured my attention was II Corinthians 4:8-10: "We are hard pressed on every side, but not crushed; perplexed, but not in despair; persecuted, but not abandoned; struck down, but not destroyed. We always carry around in our body the death of Jesus, so that the life of Jesus may also be revealed in our body."

This passage captivated my heart, though I could not say why. Now finally after having called on this scripture almost as a motto for 20 years, I understood its significance.

Sometimes as ministers of the gospel of God, we hide our afflictions, thinking perhaps that they might do some harm to the church. We don't realize that our afflictions might be of benefit to the church.

To be honest implies being realistic as well – confronting reality even when it's difficult to accept. First, when afflictions come, we have to accept that they are real. We have a tendency to want to hide them even from our wife and children so they won't suffer. Our afflictions cause us pain and we want to cry and we do cry. This sincerity of emotion should cause us to ponder. Whereas it is part of the privilege of our calling to carry the burdens of others, who is there to carry our burdens?

Being a pastor is the best job I could imagine. And yet as a minister of the gospel, I am not in any way superior to anyone else just because I have answered this calling of God. When sickness hits me, I get weak just like everyone else. I cry with my human pain and weakness; I get physically and emotionally exhausted. Through my wife's illness, I experienced all of these frailties and feelings. Despite all of it, if able, we still have to carry on the work God has put in our hands. We may feel all alone while we're going about this work in the midst of our affliction. We might feel like no one can possibly understand what we're going through. We might even invoke that famous exclamation Christ uttered on the cross, "My God, why have you forsaken me?"

Regardless of what some people might think, God's faithful workers, pastors included, are not exempt from problems in life. We get tired, worn out and maybe even more so than most people because of the great amount of time we spend feeding our sheep spiritually and not having a human pastor of our own to nourish us.

All the workers of God have trials and burdens – all of us: Christian workers, pastors, missionaries – every servant of God. We may wonder and ask ourselves and God, "Why is this happening to me?" But the fact of the matter is it happens to us all. It is the will of God that all those who serve him prove themselves faithful through times of anguish and tribulation. Paul, one of the greatest men of God and fully faithful to Christ, had more than his share. He was on death row, alone, poor, without protection, sick – but he stood firm in his faith (II Timothy 4:6-8). Do we deserve better than Paul?

Look at what the Lord advises us in II Timothy 2:3, "Endure hardship with us like a good soldier of Christ Jesus." Service to the Lord is compared with military service – a soldier in combat. And Christ's death on the cross has assured our victory.

God's workers must preach the gospel, looking for souls to love and save, without allowing our problems to dilute the message of salvation to the lost. Christ is our example. He suffered as a man in the work to which he was assigned by God. So must we. We're not angels – we're just human. This is our course. Christ said, "If anyone would come after me, he must deny himself and take up his cross and follow me," Matthew 16:24.

Though I might feel alone sometimes, I'm not. I'm in excellent company with the great men of God who have gone through the same if not worse: Job, Jeremiah, Moses, Elijah. All of them were tempted to quit. Jonah even ran from his ministry.

Problems mean struggle and struggle means life. While we have life, Satan will continually put himself in our path, but God will give us the victory. Through Jesus we are more than conquerors, as the word tells us.

"My prayer is not that you take them out of this world but that you protect them from the evil one," John 17:15. May I suggest you read that entire passage beginning from John 17:9 through 26?

Answers to Prayer

While Udelia suffered with her kidneys, I wasn't able to eat many things or drink any carbonated soda. Even fruit and vegetables aggravated my ulcer. After breakfast, my stomach would swell and I had to take several medicines to combat the acid in my stomach. I thought about living life like that and just couldn't imagine it.

I began to pray for my health and Jesus gave me the answer. God healed my ulcer and my depression. I underwent some tests in a hospital in Santiago and when I traveled to Lima, I had another endoscopy, as well as a biopsy. Happily, they did not find anything and with some natural remedies, God healed me – a wondrous work of the Lord.

$$\approx$$

Many brothers and sisters throughout the United States and in Latin America continued in pray for Udelia and our family. In the last week of January 2000, Udelia had a dream. A man dressed in white, and one other man beside him, were taking her to surgery.

When she woke, she said, "Narciso, Jesus visited me last night about my kidney. The Lord has a kidney for me, glory to God." She then prayed thanking God for the kidney – she was so secure in her gratitude, such a strong faith that God had a kidney for her.

Later that day, we received a visit from some friends from Santiago, Brother Rodolfo and his wife. They comforted Udelia telling her that the Lord would provide a kidney for her.

Udelia responded, "Yes, the kidney is ready for me. Jesus told me."

Her confident answer frankly surprised our visitors.

≈

On February 12, Udelia got up early, as she usually does, and went to the dialysis center. As she did every time, she asked God to help her bear the pain. They hooked Udelia up to the dialysis machine at 8:00 a.m. and as the machine started removing her blood and cleaning it, she fell asleep. An hour later, a doctor came up to her and very gently woke her up and told her there was a kidney ready for her.

Udelia was speechless at first, then finally said, "I knew that Jesus had one for me." Then she thanked the doctor.

Udelia's Testimony – In Her Own Words

"It was a Saturday morning. I woke up at 5:40 a.m., the same time I woke every time I had to go to dialysis. I had a cup of tea with some cookies and then the van arrived to take me to the center.

I said good-bye to my husband, got in the van with the other six patients going to the center. When we arrived, the nurses were ready to connect us to the machines by sticking big needles – so thick they look like knitting needles – into our veins. The machine pumped our blood out, passed it over a cleaning disk then returned it to the body. On this day, I fell asleep within a few minutes of beginning dialysis.

About an hour later, the doctor on duty woke me and told me he had news. He said, 'Udelia, they just called me from the transplant center. There's a kidney for you! We have to advise your husband to come pick you up and take you there.'

I didn't speak; I didn't even breathe. I was so grateful to God. It had only been a month and a half since I signed up for the transplant program. Jesus answered my prayers so quickly.

They called my husband several times, but there was no answer. It happened to be the day when vacation Bible school was starting and Narciso was out with the kids at church. The doctor called the police and asked them to go find him urgently. We only had four hours to arrive at the hospital where the kidney was waiting.

I wracked my brain for a neighbor's phone number and suddenly came up with Brother Gregorio's number, giving it to the doctor. His wife Marta answered the phone. She went to tell my husband and then also called my son Eliezer.

Eliezer was so happy he grabbed a jacket and headed out running in the rain. He said his jacket was waving over his head like a flag and that suited him fine – he was so happy that there was a kidney for his mother.

The police found Narciso on the highway on his way already. Within half an hour, he was at the center. I was ready and waiting for him when he arrived and we left in a hurry to get to the transplant center. He drove faster than 120 kilometers per hour; what's worse, it was a rainy day. Nevertheless, we wanted to get to the center before the kidney was no longer useful.

We made it and were soon in the prep room. The surgery lasted five hours.

The whole experience was the most dramatic thing that ever happened to me. Though exhilarating, it was also quite difficult. I was disappointed by the initial results – the new kidney was only functioning at 30 percent capacity. I was depressed and cried a lot. When Narciso visited me in the hospital I would say, 'The kidney is a gift from God and it doesn't work.'

We continued praying and after eight days, the kidney started to work very well. And now it works perfectly. I can eat anything, drink plenty of water, walk, work – it's truly a miracle of God. It seems Jesus must still want me in his service.

I am so thankful to the hundreds of brothers and sisters who prayed for me – praying in support of my own petition that God would grant a miracle. For 19 months God permitted me to live with failed kidneys. The entire time I was dependent on a dialysis machine. God permitted this trial because it has a good purpose for me.

I want to encourage my Christian family to not faint when you are in trials and tests. Jesus has the answer. He is the same yesterday, today and tomorrow. I want to die serving my Master who has done so many good things and given so many good things to me."

No End to the Obstacles

My wife has had almost constant health problems since the day she first went to the doctor with the kidney problem back in 1994. She has continued to have kidney infections that often result in hospitalization – sometimes for a few days, sometimes more. Recently, she was hospitalized for 13 days. Her treatments are harsh and humiliating and she is often mistreated in the hospital, as are others. There seems to be no recourse – she is just at the mercy of the hospital staff. Yet we pray to God who knows all and will have his justice.

Through it all, Udelia remains faithful to God and grateful for life. She is most grateful that she has lived long enough to see her sons grow to manhood and begin their own ministries in the Lord's work. To say that she has been undaunted by all the tragedy and tribulation of her life, however, would be inaccurate. All that has happened to her has made her fearful – sometimes to do things as simple as ride in a car or stay at home alone.

Perhaps as much or more so than her health, Udelia's childhood has contributed to the emotional battles she has faithfully fought throughout her life. Udelia is a private person and was reluctant to open up about much of her childhood for many years. We had been married a long time before she told me even part of her experiences. From what she has told me, I know that she suffered severe abuse as a young girl and becoming a mother at a very early age was a result of some of that abuse. Her story is disturbing, but important to tell for a couple of reasons. Foremost, it is her reality – to brush over her past with casual references seems a form of denial. Secondly, and something that Udelia has recently grown to understand, is that her testimony can be of great help and inspiration to others who suffered similar abuses.

Before she was even born, Udelia's natural father died, at age 50. Soon after Udelia was born, her mother remarried. Udelia had three older sisters, but by the time she was eight, the number was down to one. Two of her sisters died at ages 13 and 15 of tuberculosis. Udelia remembers that they had faith in their salvation. One told her that she was going to a place where they would be waiting for her with a white robe and she would be very happy there. Those were her sister's last words to the eight-year-old Udelia.

Udelia's remaining sister was 18-years-old when the other sisters passed away and soon she left home to live in Lima. In fact, the whole family left their home. Udelia, her mother and stepfather went into the mountains to live and there they were wheat farmers and raised cattle.

To say that Udelia suffered at home with her violent mother and stepfather would be an understatement. Once when Udelia was only 10 years old, just for letting a donkey get loose, Udelia's mother beat her and then strung her up with a rope around her neck. She might have died there if the neighbors hadn't intervened and released her from the cord that was choking her and had already bloodied her neck. On another occasion, when Udelia's teachers reported to her mother that Udelia had not been doing some of her homework, her mother beat her so badly it broke her leg. Yet Udelia never had time to dedicate to her studies because she was worked constantly at home.

Then one time, Udelia was bringing home a horse packed with wheat from the field and the animal got spooked. As it took off, Udelia became tangled in the rope and the horse dragged her on the rocky ground for quite a distance. Her entire body was cut and bruised and when her mother saw what had happened, she remarked that it was a good thing that she would now know how to lead a horse.

Her stepfather was no better. Every time he came home, he would beat both mother and daughter until he was exhausted. Udelia shook in fear the entire time he stayed at home.

Udelia's mother and stepfather had another daughter and she was treated quite differently. The father would bring home sweets for her, warning Udelia that they were not for her and if she touched them, he would kill her. This was Udelia's life until she was old enough to go live with her sister in Lima and go to high school.

~~~

A couple of years ago, when I was in Lima visiting my parents, I decided to look up Udelia's daughter who was then in her late 30's and had four children of her own. I had not seen her for some time and she was quite changed. She was bitter and mad at God, the church and her mother. I asked her forgiveness for any part of the hurt I may have caused her.

That day she told me the story of her beginnings, to the extent that she knew, and it was all new information to me. She said she was sure that her mother hadn't wanted to have her and her brother because they were both the products of rape. She understood that the child of a rape can be disdained in a sense.

I have asked Udelia about the rapes, but I can only imagine those would be terrible memories for her to relive through recounting — and she won't.

~~~

In September 2006, we got a call from California. It was Udelia's niece. Both of Udelia's sisters, the older and the younger stepsister, now live in California. I passed the phone to Udelia and watched as she responded in both fearful surprise and happiness. Her sister was apologizing to her. When she hung up, she went to the bedroom and began to cry with heavy sobs, saying "Thank God, the monster who ruined my life is dead."

Then she opened up a bit. When she had gone to Lima to attend high school, she lived with her sister and her sister's husband. One day, her sister took Udelia to an office and put her in it. Udelia's brother-in-law was there waiting. He beat her and raped her, and she became pregnant with her first child. Udelia was only 15 years old. Her brother-in-law was sentenced to prison for two years for his crime.

I can only speculate that Udelia's sister knowingly, though perhaps not willingly, was an accomplice to this cruel and violent crime because she herself had been a victim of an abusive childhood and was at the time victim to that heinous spouse.

When the rapist got out of prison, he and a friend went looking for Udelia. The friend lured Udelia into a store by saying a friend of hers was waiting and needed her help. What she found instead was her brother-in-law, fresh out of jail, wanting revenge and this time, with a gun. He raped Udelia again as she screamed for help. And bewilderingly, she became pregnant once again by this evil man.

Udelia had no family to support her. She hated her mother and sister. A kind woman who sold vegetables took pity on her and gave her lodging. Some time later, she met her uncles, brothers to her real father, and they took her in and helped her and never deserted her.

From that point on, until that phone call last September, Udelia never spoke to her sister again. Now her sister was calling to ask forgiveness for being an accomplice to the first rape. Her sister also told her that the man who raped her was dead. Both of Udelia's sisters are now Christians and members of the Assemblies of God.

These experiences have impacted every facet of Udelia's life – in both negative and positive ways. As she always says, thank God she found Christ. She reads the Bible and prays daily and this has been her main tool for survival – emotionally and spiritually.

Udelia loves all her children, but she can't help but wish the first two had not been conceived in violence. She prays for them and their families daily, that they will come to know God and serve him. In fact, her son is a pastor in Argentina. We don't hear much from him, but he and Gerson are in more frequent contact through e-mail.

Another profound effect Udelia's early years had on her was to make her a protective mother of Gerson and Eliezer. Quite obviously because of all my "walking" for Jesus, my wife had the primary responsibility of caring for our sons at all times. Udelia has been an excellent mother and she ushered both our boys through adolescence with great wisdom. Not until that phone call some months ago did I understand Udelia's full motivation for being a wonderful mother.

Udelia has been a true partner in my entire ministry. I'm quite sure I haven't given her enough credit in these pages for all the details she saw to in the day-to-day administration of the many churches we've planted. The simple fact that she has been willing to go to these great distances with me is confirmation that her calling is as strong as my own and God has used her just as gloriously – and continues to do so.

Discussion Primers

Now that you know more about Udelia, reevaluate your answers to the primer from page 55. Many Christians have a victorious walk despite scars like those left by Udelia's traumatic childhood. Even as Udelia has accomplished much in Christ's name, she has also suffered from the residual effects of her childhood. How can we have a victorious life through Christ despite painful events that have shaped our lives and forged our personalities?

Gerson Makes His Decision

After finishing the obligatory three years of high school, Gerson elected to stay on a fourth year and study music at English College, his high school. Throughout his senior year, we spoke to him about his future. My wife recommended to him that he study in a university, perhaps history or journalism. He was undecided and we felt the need to pray for God to direct him.

One day in a family meeting, Gerson announced to us that he had decided to study theology. It was quite a surprise to all of us and my wife even tried several times to discourage him from this course.

She said, "Son, we have suffered greatly in God's work. There's never enough money. If you want to study theology, won't you at least go first to the university?"

Some months went by and Gerson announced again. "I've decided to study theology in some seminary and I need to get some information. I have made up my mind and I know God will provide the money for my studies. I want to dedicate my youth to Christ and if my God allows it, later I will study some other profession — after I finish my theology studies."

Gerson's mind was set. God had called him to the ministry and how could we oppose that? We thanked God that he was ready to enlist in spiritual service.

That year I made a trip to Costa Rica for the Inter-American Conference and while there, I visited the Universidad Bíblica Latinoamericana (Latin American Bible University) and the Nazarene University. I discovered that the cost for Gerson to study there would be prohibitive.

Upon my return, I made a trip to Lima and visited the Escuela de Teología Superior — Seminario Andino (Andean Seminary,

Advanced School of Theology). I brought the materials from that school back to Gerson and we wrote for materials to seminaries in Ecuador, Argentina and Bolivia, as well. Gerson decided to study in Lima. Sister Hilda Rodriguez was helpful in making contact with the school and getting Gerson's application and financial aid package started.

On December 15, 1998, Gerson's dream became reality as he said good-bye to his mother. Udelia cried as he left, but she was happy, particularly knowing he would be staying with family in Lima; he was going to stay at Udelia's older daughter Zara's house. Eliezer and I went with Gerson to Peru and we bought him a bed, table, chair and a small armoire and placed them in his room at Zara's house.

Then we went to the seminary and visited with the director. Gerson would have to take an aptitude test, which he passed with no difficulty. With Gerson settled in Lima, Eliezer and I caught a plane back to Chile. We said our good-byes at the airport. Gerson was sad to be alone and away from his family for the first time.

On the plane Eliezer said, "It's boring to travel without Gerson."

At that moment I realized that Eliezer was going to greatly miss his brother, too. Beginning the next morning at home, Eliezer went through a time of tribulation. As he was leaving the house in the morning he would say, "I want to see my brother, Gerson. I hope he comes on the bus today."

My wife and I became so concerned about him that we took him to the hospital. He seemed sick from missing his brother so much. We assured him that soon classes would start and he would get involved with his friends again and everything would be all right.

Eliezer insisted, "My friends aren't my brother. I miss my brother."

But sure enough, once school started up and he had studies and friends to focus on, he started to grow accustomed to being the only child at home.

While Eliezer suffered at home with us in Chile, Gerson was suffering alone in Lima – missing both his parents and brother. He spent five months crying alone in his room. He would walk through the streets alone looking for a church to attend. He finally found the

Christian and Missionary Alliance and got involved there. He worked there for two years with the youth and even started a new work with that church.

On weekends, he would get together with his Uncle Elindor who encouraged him.

Even though Gerson was somewhat familiar with Peruvian culture – being originally from there and having been raised by Peruvian parents, he had more to learn in Lima. He was assaulted several times during his theology studies in Lima. Thieves stole his backpack full of books, his Bible, and on another occasion, they tried stealing his backpack again at knife point. That time, looking the crooks in the face, he slowly took out a tract and offered it to them, encouraging them to accept Jesus into their hearts. As Gerson spoke of the Word of God, the crook put his knife down and quickly scooted off.

Gerson says that in Peru, you have to exercise your faith – actually live by faith.

Gerson's convictions for Christ are a wonder to me, and as his father, I feel great pride in the man he proved himself to be during his studies. He attended the Andean Seminary in Lima for four years, finally earning his bachelor's degree in Bible literature. In the mornings, he studied English in a language school and on the weekends and some evenings, he attended and later began to preach at the Christian and Missionary Alliance in a neighborhood known as San Juan Marcías Callao.

During his vacations, he would come home and work in the ministry in Chile, organizing and directing summer camps. God blessed Gerson with many opportunities to gain practical experience working with youth and also in the church while he prepared himself academically.

Gerson graduated from the Andean Seminary in December 2002. He sent me an e-mail advising me of the date and time, also asking that I attend. Udelia was still unable to make such a long trip, but she insisted, "Narciso, you have to be at our son's graduation."

Gerson had also invited the pastor of the Christian and Missionary Alliance, as well as many of the youth group, to attend his graduation. The night of the graduation, the graduates filed in wearing blue gowns and Gerson was the youngest of all the students. First there was a church service, then the graduation. Each graduate received a medal and a diploma. The director handed out the diplomas, but the graduate got to choose who would put the medal on him.

As our last name starts with a "Z," Gerson was practically last in line to get his diploma. I was overcome emotionally seeing my oldest son up front getting his bachelor's degree. As Gerson received his diploma, they announced, "The person who will present his medal will be his father, Pastor Narciso Zamora." At that moment, I was the happiest man alive – seeing my son as a servant of God.

When I got up to the stage and took the medal to put around Gerson's neck, the director said to me, "Pastor Zamora…"

I looked at her and then gave her a big hug. She had been a member of the first church I ever pastored back when I was in the Bible institute! Now she was the director of a whole university program. If possible, it made my heart even happier.

After the ceremony, we took photos and then went to my sister Ana's home to rest. But not for long. The next morning, we left early so Gerson could get to church and preach.

Gerson's next move was to start a master's program in Bible sciences at the Latin American Bible University in San Jose, Costa Rica. After finishing that degree, in December 2004, Gerson returned home to Chile and worked as a pastor in the church at Isla de Maipo during 2005 and until June 2006. Gerson decided to return to Lima, Peru, to continue his studies in theology, pursuing a terminal degree in theology, which he completed in June 2007.

God Calls Eliezer

Eliezer decided not to go to college after high school. He really didn't know what to do. He lacked direction – he didn't want to study any more but he didn't feel ready to start to work, either.

"Gerson, study to be a pastor and I will work to give you my tithes so you can survive. I'm just going to be a little brother in the church," were the words Eliezer often said to Gerson while he attended seminary.

My wife and I prayed each day, asking the Lord Jesus to call Eliezer to his service like he had done with Gerson. Eli, as we call him now, wanted to be a Sunday school teacher. This made us very happy. So we enrolled him in a Methodist facility to study on Saturdays. He went for three Saturdays and then said, "I don't want to study theology ever again."

He started preparing himself for college – getting ready to take college entrance exams.

We spent a great deal of time and energy preparing Eliezer for his exams and when he finally took them, he came up short of the points he needed to enter college.

He was hit hard with the news and reacted by running away from home. He left a note on the table saying, "I'm leaving home and not coming back. Don't worry, Momma, I'll be fine."

We didn't find the letter until night time and when we read it, Udelia started crying and we both got down on our knees. We prayed for Eli, for God to take care of him wherever he was. It occurred to me at that moment that many years previously, I had done the same thing to my parents. I ran away from home and left my parents to cry. I believed I was being paid back for my own foolish deed. I accepted it, asked forgiveness and prayed that Eli would come home and serve the Lord.

In the middle of that very night, we got a phone call from Eli. My wife answered. He was asking forgiveness for what he had done and said that if we would have him back, he would come back. My wife was so happy to hear his voice.

In the morning, we waited and finally we got another phone call. Eli was afraid to come home because of what he had done. I talked with him and encouraged him that we wanted him to come home. When he arrived home, it was like the parable of the prodigal son from the gospel of Luke was being played out in our home.

~~~

We didn't know what would happen with Eli, whether he would study or work. We just dedicated the matter to prayer. Eli was allowing himself to be influenced heavily by his peers and, little by little, he got into the hip-hop movement – and that created a lot of problems.

In June 2000, we were having a service in a neighborhood called El Bosque, in Santiago, when a young man who had heart problems came up, got on his knees and accepted Christ through his tears. That day, God also touched Eli's heart and called him to God's service. Eliezer was moved by the Holy Spirit. He became a different young man. He started learning to play the guitar and sing in church. He would feel the presence of God as he sang. One night at a prayer vigil, in tears, Eliezer announced that God was calling him to serve him and God was transforming him.

One night at home with just the three of us, Eli announced that he had decided to study music. We told him it would be hard to make a living with just music, and we kept praying for him.

Finally that November, he decided to study theology. At first, it did not seem likely, but then he persisted in finding a place to study. We thought about Ecuador. We got some information about various schools and also information on the Bible University of Santa Cruz, Bolivia. Eli himself wrote to the director of the Boa Terra

Bible Institute in Curitiba, Brazil. When he received a response, he said, "This is the place I should study." We were surprised by the decision and tried to explain to him that the language would present a problem.

He replied, "I'm going to enroll at the Brazilian Institute to learn Portuguese."

We went one morning to Santiago with Eli to enroll him and pay for the one-month intensive course of study. He was afraid of wasting our money and so he tried hard with Portuguese. The time passed and in February 2001, he announced, "It's time for me to travel to the seminary."

It started to seem real now that he would leave. He packed his bags and got all his documentation in order for traveling and enrolling in the seminary. My wife was happy that Eli had truly decided to serve the Lord. He didn't seem to have any fear of studying and living in another culture and with another language. He left with Bible and guitar in hand.

He took the bus to Buenos Aires, Argentina, and stayed a week there with our old friends, José Luis and Sonia. He had a wonderful time! Then, by himself, he traveled on to Curitiba, Brazil. That's where the wonder ended. His first months were a real struggle. He didn't know the language well – just some introductory phrases – and the culture was so different. He said he felt like a hermit.

Isolated, he started to miss his family and at one point said to himself, "What am I doing here, alone, without knowing the language? Why am I here?" At just this time of discouragement, he received a letter from me.

I had written, "Eli, be strong. Be brave, very brave. Jesus has called you. He will help you and give you all you need. Don't give up, stay firm in the Lord. This is your first test. Go forward with the Lord."

After he finished the letter, he was determined to stick out these first difficult days in the service of the Lord. He eventually got used to his new environment and he really got into his studies and into learning about the lives that God has used throughout history.

〰

Eliezer learned Portuguese! He spent three years in the Boa Terra Bible Institute preparing himself for the ministry in the service of our Lord Jesus. His mother and I were very happy as we saw that he was dedicated to studying. He came and went from our house during vacation, back to Curitiba and he never seemed to tire of it. He had high energy and a love for his Lord and his studies. Each time he would come home on vacation, he had new things to share – new things he had learned and Bible messages that were highly relevant to today for our youth and the church.

≈

In 2002, Eli fell in love with a young lady, Cristiani, from Panambí, Brazil. She finished her studies at Boa Terra two years before Eli. The two of them started to pray that God would unite their lives within a year, and if not, that they would simply be good friends.

One day I got a letter: "Papa, I have become engaged to a young lady who serves the Lord and I am hoping to marry her."

I was not happy to hear the news. It didn't matter to me if she was a Christian or a preacher or anything else. All that was well and good, but I couldn't wrap my mind around Eliezer getting married at this time. It just didn't fit for me – not in my head nor my heart. The problem, however, was that Eliezer could marry with or without his father's blessing. He was more than 5,000 kilometers away!

Udelia thought it was a joke at first, but then she prayed every day about Eli's decision.

Alone in my office, I prayed to the Lord to know what to do. I had always been opposed to my sons marrying young. I had always hoped they would finish their studies, get a little older and then marry. But it didn't happen that way with Eli.

He decided to get married just after he finished his theology studies. After they made their decision, my wife and I prayed that they would remain together their entire lives and serve the Lord together. What we were concerned about was whether the young woman Eli had chosen was ready to leave home, preach and suffer for Christ. I discussed it with my friends, telling them he really needed a woman who would love him and dedicate herself to serve Jesus with all her heart — not fearing travel to any part of the world, with or without money.

When all was said and done, we simply had to accept with fear and trembling the decision they had made, support it and help them out as best we could.

〜〜〜

The day of Eliezer's graduation was approaching. He asked me to attend the graduation and then to preside over his and Cristiani's wedding.

In November 2003, I traveled from Santiago to Mendoza, Argentina, and from there on another bus to Resistencia, Argentina. Then I took another bus to Iguazu, which is on the border between Argentina and Brazil. In Iguazu, I stopped for the night and got a bath and a good night's sleep. It had been a 36-hour trip already. When I passed over into Brazil, I bought a ticket to Curitiba, catching a taxi to the station where the buses leave for Iguazu Falls. I was able to see and enjoy the falls, which are a wonder from God.

That night I took the bus to Curitiba and arrived the next morning at 8:00 a.m. As I stepped off the bus, I saw Eli with his friend Marcos, waiting for me to take me to the dormitories of the seminary. Curitiba was quite a surprise to me with its many modern buildings and clean and well-organized streets.

When we got to Boa Terra, Eli introduced me to the assistant director, Brother Ibo. Then Eli's friends arrived, all the people he had studied with those three years. They were already nostalgic because in just two days everything would be over and they would part ways — some for a long time, others for life.

The day of Eli's graduation was November 29, 2003. It was a marvelous celebration among many different congregations of churches. Many brothers and pastors came from São Paulo and the auditorium was full. At 8:00 p.m., all the professors and pastors in attendance filed into the auditorium. I felt blessed to be among them. Then there was silence and as the music started, the graduates in their black robes started to file in.

There was an opening prayer, some hymns, some remarks by professors and then the main message. The director, Reverend Nelson Yunges, gave each of the graduates a diploma. At the end, there were many tears as people said good-bye. It was the end of their first accomplishment as adults and as servants in the work of Christ. It was the beginning of a career that knows no end. With eyes only on Jesus, they would be more than conquerors.

After the graduation, I asked Eli and Cristiani to please find another minister to marry them, as I assumed the customs in Brazil were probably so different and it would be better if a local minister married them. But they had already made up their minds. I was to marry them.

〰

A few days later Eliezer told me, "Papa, I have to go to Panambí to help with the preparations for the wedding. Do you want to go with me or stay here in Curitiba?

I replied, "Just where do you think I would stay if I don't go with you?"

"In my mother-in-law's house," he said.

"Oh, son, I don't want to be any trouble for your mother-in-law. Why don't you go to a local church and find a place for me to stay," I suggested.

Cristiani called the pastor of the Lutheran church and asked if I might stay with him. He agreed. So I stayed in Curitiba for a week with Fabio and Miriam, the pastor and his wife – a wonderful couple. Two days before the wedding, Fabio took me to the bus station and saw me off for Panambí.

Eliezer and his soon-to-be brother-in-law were waiting where the bus let me off on the main road to Panambí. We went to meet my future daughter-in-law.

My first words to Cristiani were, "Are you committed to suffering for Christ?"

She replied with certainty and an affirmative nod, "Yes."

With that answer I was content to have the tea and bread with jam that they offered me.

Later my son took me to his room and asked me, "Papa, are you happy with my fiancee?"

I said, "I'm neither happy nor sad. The important thing is that you love her and she loves you."

〰〰

Later we went to the local pastor's house. I spent most of Friday with him chatting about his work and ministry, and on Saturday we visited a rehabilitation center. I also spent considerable time in prayer for our families.

On December 13, 2003, we celebrated the wedding in the evening with many people from the local congregation attending. After the wedding ceremony, all of Cristiani's friends said good-bye to her, many with tears. It was a cause for celebration but also for nostalgia.

〰〰

I started back for Chile on Christmas Day at 5:00 a.m. In the midst of a torrential downpour, Brother Dos Santos took me to Uruguayana, which is on the border with Argentina. I made it through immigration then went to a bus terminal called Los Libres (The Free Ones), which is a very dangerous place. Many gangs of disenfranchised youth from Paraguay come in there on buses to cause trouble and rob people.

I took an old bus to Resistencia. It was still raining and water was leaking through everywhere on the bus. I got to Resistencia at 10:00 p.m. and one hour later, I was on my way to Mendoza. The trip lasted all night, the next day and next night, and we finally got to Mendoza at 6:00 a.m. the following day. From there, I was on yet another bus to Santiago, Chile, and I finally arrived there at 4:00 p.m.

Eliezer and Cristiani arrived four days later, having traveled with

11 boxes of their personal belongings all the way to Santiago, Chile, from Panambí, Brazil.

When we all got rested up, we conducted the wedding ceremony again in Chile. Many of Eli's Chilean friends also wanted to participate in his wedding. For this event, Pastor Victor Quispe and his family and Ann and Herb Morgan from Texas were special guests and were made the honorary masters of ceremony for the wedding.

Eli and Cristiani moved in next door to Udelia and me. On our property, we have two houses; the one the kids moved into was the original house we built and had vacated when we added on a larger, two-story house to the property.

Eli and Cristiani helped in the local ministries, getting some practical experiences while they prepared themselves, in more ways than one, to go to Valparaíso and finally start in earnest the church there. The work in Valparaíso had been struggling to get off the ground since my first weeks in Chile, back in 1989.

We had many problems with the Valparaíso church. The Clifton Avenue Church of God in Ohio helped us purchase a property for a church in Valparaíso where we already had an active group under the direction of Jose Aburto. We asked Jose to facilitate the real estate transaction for the property purchase. Later, when we saw the notarized papers, we realized the land had been put in his name – not the name of the church.

The sponsoring church's pastor, Sam Wollum, told us, "The deed must be in the name of the Church of God and not of any one person."

When the remaining money arrived to complete the purchase, we corrected the situation and it infuriated Jose Aburto. He came to see me with his brother-in-law with the intention of beating me up and even threatened that if he had possessed a knife, he would have killed "that Zamora."

Brother Arias and others helped defend us against the threats of those two angry men.

Instead of hurting us physically, this disgruntled Jose Aburto went on a campaign to ruin us and knocked on a lot of people's doors. I would have rather taken a beating!

Through it all, we continued to pray to Jesus for the victory. And we were able soon enough to get the deed and all the papers put in the name of the Church of God, but we needed new leadership there.

In September 2004, Eli and Cristiani rented a truck and drove the 270 kilometers to the coast to start their first mission work. The place we had in Valparaíso was very rustic and rundown – full of fleas and no protection against the many delinquents and drug addicts that hung around in that neighborhood. In fact, delinquents had started to use our church yard as a short cut from one block to the next – also as a convenient place to be shielded from sight as they lit their pipes.

Eli and Cristiani had their work cut out for them and it was extremely difficult. When I left my son and daughter in that situation in Valparaíso, I went home and my wife and I cried together, praying for the young couple who were already greatly missed. They had left a comfortable home that they even painted inside to their liking, to go live in a rat- and flea-infested shack in the middle of a high-crime neighborhood.

My wife cried for them every day, missing them, but thank God we were only 270 kilometers away and on weekends, I went to visit them. I helped my son sink posts and string fence to cut off the path for the drug addicts and add some security to their home. Those first weeks before the fence was up were the worst for the couple. They could hardly sleep at night for fear of having the house broken into.

With the fence up, they could sleep soundly and move on to other concerns, like visiting homes nearby and planning their first project, a vacation Bible school to stir the interest of neighborhood kids. Some 27 kids attended and many of them are still going to Sunday school in Valparaíso even now.

From there, they started going house to house evangelizing, and showing films and holding outdoor evangelism campaigns in front of the church.

When not doing that direct ministry work, they were hard at work on the property. Using a shovel and pick, they both started leveling the property, which was on a hill, by digging out the incline behind the building. The area of dirt they moved was approximately 2 meters high by 3 meters wide and 11 meters deep. It took them almost a year to get the dirt shoveled away. When they finally had all the dirt heaped up, they contracted some trucks to haul off the dirt. It took more than 30 truck loads to move all that dirt away!

Besides doing hard manual labor, Cristiani also worked in a seamstress' shop to help support the ministry. She worked there full-time and sometimes worked overtime – 12 hours a day. In Chile, foreign workers are often exploited and this was the case with Cristiani. She was paid minimum wage for her time and never paid anything extra for the overtime. She continued in that situation out of financial necessity but it took its toll on her health. She got sick and couldn't afford to go to the doctor. Health care in Chile is expensive for people who don't qualify for health benefits. God blessed us financially during that time and we were able to help Eli and Cristiani with the medical bills. She quit the seamstress job after that.

Then it was Eli's turn to go out and find a job. He started working at a used car lot. The job paid minimum wage, but as Eliezer is also a foreigner in Chile, he was also exploited and made slightly less than minimum wage, and again, nothing extra for overtime – and he often worked 12-hour days.

The couple did their ministry work primarily on the weekends.

This was their first ministry experience and it was a true test. After a little more than a year, they decided, for health concerns and because of their desperate financial situation, to move on. They were not giving up on God's work but decided to move back to Brazil to continue it. And God always blesses when we are dedicated to his work.

In October 2005, they left for Condor, a town in the south of Brazil, to start a new church. We couldn't argue with their decision and admired them for what they had endured. We held them up in prayer and supported them as best we could.

Eli and Cristiani got the work in Condor started in December 2005, and they have a small congregation, with some 30 or more people in regular attendance. They are still struggling financially be-

cause most of the new Christians there are not tithing and the giving is only sufficient to pay the occupancy costs of the building,
which serves also as their home. But Eli and Cristiani are happy
serving the Lord and leading souls to Christ. Cristiani has found a
job in a seamstress shop, enabling Eli to work full-time in the ministry. He goes house to house every weekday afternoon. Everyone
in Condor knows him, and he's heard some say that he's the only
pastor they know who visits people in their homes and evangelizes
in the streets.

≋

And what about Valparaíso? We asked a Chilean pastor, Alberto
Martínez, and his family to assume responsibility of the work in
Valparaíso. Thank God they accepted the challenge. There is cur-
rently an active congregation there with a strong core group.

Another Walkabout?

The Church of God in Chile continues to grow and God is adding souls to our numbers on a regular basis. Since arriving in Chile, our objectives have not changed. We meant to establish congregations, cultivate local leaders, purchase properties and build buildings for these congregations. God has richly blessed us and we have succeeded in purchasing three properties in the name of the Church of God. Also, we began a leadership training program similar to the one we started in Ecuador, and now we have our first class completing their preparation to work in the ministry.

We have also sent missionaries from Chile back to some of the same congregations Udelia and I pastored in Peru in the early years of our ministry.

In 2005, Udelia and I began to pray to know God's will for us in the coming years, while he gives us life and health still. We may have several decades left in us and we both want to use them for the glory of God.

We have planned a new project that we desire to see begin in 2008. As we get older, it will be impossible for us to be traveling to other countries to start new works, but what we can do is prepare workers and send them. Thus, we have the vision that is now in the Lord's spiritual laboratory and in due time will come to fruition. Our goal is to establish a school to prepare missionaries who will plant churches in Latin America. We are preparing the materials and laying the foundations for this project. We have had invitations from brothers in Argentina, Bolivia and Peru to develop this project. We are praying and continually searching for a city in Latin America that is least evangelized so we can go there, begin first a church and then a missions school.

We already have strategic locations in mind in Peru where the Christian evangelical church has not been developed. This will add to the difficulty at first, but the work is from Jesus and only he can do his work. If God guides us to that place then he will do all the work. From there, we would begin to train missionaries from all over Latin America to plant churches.

∿

In every missionary project we've worked on, we've not been alone. Of course, we have our Heavenly Father, but we have more, too. God has provided for our needs through people – people who gave us food when we were literally starving, a horse when we couldn't walk anymore, literature to use in evangelism, an opportunity to sell Bible covers, and many generous supporters who have sent money – funds that we have always tried to make the very most of. I name many of these people in my final acknowledgments and mention many others in these pages. Of course, I cannot remember them all over the span of 30-plus years of ministry. But they are in my heart's memory.

We have no firm commitments of support for our new project, but I know I can count on my God to continue to provide for our needs through people. We are partners, and united we will have the victory! Many souls will be saved of their sin. Isn't that the point of all that walking, after all?

Acknowledgments

Thank you to all my brothers and sisters all over North and South America, and some in Europe, too, who have contributed to the Zamora family ministry. I can't name them all, but here are a few I can't help but mention:

Pastor Sam and Jean Wollum and the Clifton Street Church of God; Pastor Sam and Francis Harrington and the work group he brought; Gerardo Barrantes and his wife; Pastor Larry and Rena Lautaret and the Church of God in Whitefish; Brother Lawrence, Maxine and the work group they brought; John and Rita Stein and their children; the Church of God in Marietta, Ga.; Jack Wilson; Evelyn Anderson and her son William; Donna Schillinger; Doris and William Barberena; Ann and Herb Morgan; the Church of God in Fairbanks; the Moore sisters; William and Verna Lamb; Brother Millán and his wife Dekch; Willy Kant and his wife; Dr. Patton; Sister Schrader; Maurice and Dondeena Caldwell; the Park Place Church of God; the Missionary Board; the Women of the Church of God in Argentina; Alejandro and Carmen de Francisco; Carlos and Eunice Robertson; Israel Hernandez; and the Inter-American Conference.

There are many other brothers and sisters in Christ whom I would like to thank as well, for their love and support in prayer, literature, financial support, wise advice and for their efforts. Glory be to Him that lives throughout the ages! Amen.

Afterword

Being a Missionary Wherever You Are
By Michael Cassidy

There is something very powerful about sharing what we know to be true in our own experience. The blind man whom Jesus healed didn't have great theological knowledge with which he could answer the people demanding to know, "Who is this person who opened your eyes and healed you?" He couldn't go into a whole recitation about how this Jesus must be the Messiah. He just said to them: "One thing I know. Whereas I was blind, now I see." That is very powerful indeed. And it's hard to argue with a changed life!

In Christian circles, people often speak of "giving your testimony" or "sharing a testimony." What they are talking about is telling others how you came to be a Christian, how you came to know Jesus Christ as your Savior and what difference this fact has made in your life.

Whether you aspire to a life in missions like you've read about in this book or are committed to serving the Lord without ever leaving your hometown, as Christians, we need to be able to share our testimonies, for we are all called at various times, if not all the time, to "be ready to give an answer to everyone who asks you to give the reason for the hope that you have" (1 Peter 3:15).

Overcoming Fears
I think all of us are afraid in some measure of speaking in front of

other people. It can be difficult to share the story of our lives, especially the memories of struggles and times of pain. Or perhaps we feel that our lives are just ordinary and doubt that anyone would want to listen. This may be especially true in the case of those who have been Christians for most or even all of their lives, have been spared suffering and have not done anything exceptionally bad or sinful. In consequence, they feel that no one will be moved by a testimony that is uninteresting. These are common fears, but as Christians we are commanded by our Lord not to worry or fear. "Fear not," says Jesus, for he is with us. And that is a great comfort.

Though we need to exercise discretion in exactly what we share, with whom and in what situations, we may often find people in our "audience" have had similar commonplace experiences or if experiencing trials are comforted and encouraged to discover they are not alone – to know that someone else has struggled with what they have faced and has found an answer, in spite of deep hurts or traumatic experiences. And for those who feel that their life experiences are unexceptional, I want to say that no one's life is without interest to others – you are sharing your "story" and people are interested in stories that are true, just as the story you just read captured your heart and attention. Besides, you will likely find that many people also feel their lives are unremarkable and, therefore, will connect with you. They may think, "Hey, this person has lived a pretty normal life, and so have I. But he found a good answer in Jesus and is living a meaningful and rich life – maybe I can too!"

Three Ingredients

Now, let's think about the three basic ingredients that go into sharing our testimony.

The first is – What life was like before I found Christ.

The second is – How I found Christ.

The third is – What life has been like since I found Christ.

In all of this the key principle is to be honest. Say what you were actually like before. If you think you were terrible, say so. If you weren't, then just be real!

I would also like to encourage you to be as specific as you can in what you share with people. If you have had some real traumas in the past, then while using wisdom in sharing, also try not to be vague about it. If someone says: "When I was a teenager, I drifted far from God and did bad things" then people wonder what those bad things were. No one can really connect with a statement like this because we have all done bad things, ranging from telling a fib to theft or slander and on and on. If we aren't specific, people won't know if their lives connect with ours or not. If we say: "When I was a teenager, I was sexually immoral, smoked pot and stole a car from my neighbor and crashed it," then people who have done similar things can connect with you and say: "Hey, I also did things like that; maybe Jesus can help me, too!" That's life before you found Christ.

Next, share exactly how you found Christ. How did it take place? I have a fairly decisive testimony; I can identify the very moment I gave my life to Christ. But my wife, Carol, says her conversion was not at all dramatic because she can never remember a time when Jesus was not real to her. There was no single, exact point in her life where she could say, "It was then that I accepted the Lord." For her, it was a process that began in childhood, even before she had any solid memories, and carried through as she grew and matured. There is no point in her trying to create a testimony that would be the same as mine. We share our own experiences and stories – no more, no less.

What has life been like since Jesus came into your heart? Some people, especially those with more lurid pasts, spend most of their testimony time telling about how awful they were and all the terrible things they did before they were a Christian. Then they give much less attention to how they became a Christian and end up saying, in effect, that they've lived happily ever after! We should aim at devoting at least one-third of our testimony to telling people what our life has been like, and then how it has been different with Jesus. This is vitally important – we want to give people an idea of what Jesus can actually do in a person's life, without exaggerating or embellishing.

If your life since conversion to Christ has been dramatic, then say so. If it hasn't been dramatic, we can say something like "I haven't had any great emotional feelings or anything like that, but what I have experienced is a deep sense of peace in my heart." Or how about:"At work I am doing better. I still have problems at the of-fice, but things are going better than they were." Or:"My wife and I are relating to each other much better. We still have our ups and downs, but our marriage is picking up." We probably still can't say: "Our marriage is absolutely blissful and everything is transformed. We never have a tiff." If that is true, of course, say so. But don't say it if it's not true. Otherwise people might just say:"She's had a great conversion but is still a liar!"

In reality, when people come to Christ, a whole new set of bat-tles and struggles often begin. I remember leading a girl to the Lord many years ago whose parents' marriage broke up the day after she became a Christian. She went through unbelievable trauma. She just couldn't put it together – coming to Jesus and then this whole thing. Jesus speaks of situations like this in the parable of the sower where the Bible says that, right after the seed is sown, the birds come swooping down to try and get it away. The Devil tries to get us to forget about Jesus and return to our old ways. If we had severe struggles right after we came to Jesus, or even at any point in our Christian lives, it's good to share this in our testimonies, as it helps prepare our listeners for such an event in their own lives.

Using Understandable Language

If we have been Christians for a significant amount of time, we can fall into speaking a sort of "Christian-ese" or jargon without being aware of it. Thus, people might speak about when they "received Jesus as their personal Savior." This is a Christian cliché with which non-Christians might not be familiar. Rather say something like: "Since I came to see that Jesus is who he said he was, I have handed my life over to him." Instead of saying:"I felt the Holy Spirit con-victing me of my sins" one might say:"I felt like God was telling me that what I was doing was wrong and that I needed to change." We have to put it in our own words and make sure these words will be understandable by people who aren't familiar with the Bible or with Christian faith.

Talk about Jesus Christ

It can be easy when sharing our testimonies to speak rather vaguely of what "God" has done in our lives rather than what "Jesus" has done. To us as Christians, of course, Jesus is God. But when speaking to someone or a group of people who are not Christians, using the word "God" can allow them to insert their own ideas about who God is – to them he could be the Buddha, Allah, the Force, a Higher Power or whatever. But if we say "Jesus" or "Christ" or "Jesus Christ", then we leave no doubt in the hearer's mind of whom we are speaking. Our testimonies are about our encounter with the God and Father of our Lord Jesus Christ. That must be clear.

Write It Down

There is real value in writing down your testimony, whether in outline form or word-for-word. Obviously there will be many different situations in which you might be called to give your testimony. You might be sitting next to someone on a bus or on an airplane and have occasion to share your story with them. In that instance, you would share it informally and conversationally. But if you were speaking to a group of people, you would probably use your notes and give a more prepared talk. If you have written down your testimony, your thoughts are in a clear order that will serve you well in any situation. It's good to refine your story so that you can give it in five or ten minutes.

Share It with Someone

When you have completed preparing your testimony, you might like to share it with a good Christian friend just for practice and get some helpful input. You might also like to share your testimony with a fellowship or Bible study group to which you belong. While a testimony is a wonderful tool for bringing non-Christians to Christ, it is also a tremendous encouragement to fellow Christians. You could also let your pastor know you would be willing to share your testimony either in church or in some kind of outreach function. I also encourage pastors to consider having persons give their testimonies regularly in church services and other functions, whether every week or once a month. It is a wonderful way of developing the skills and gifts of lay people. It is also great to hear the testimonies of people from different professions and backgrounds, i.e., lawyers, doctors, teachers, etc.

How to Lead Someone to Christ

Now that we've got our testimony organized and clearly in mind, are we ready to put it to work for the glory of God?

We often face the challenge of evangelizing, or leading someone else to Christ, with strong hesitation or even fear. "The unconverted" loom large in our minds, much like a Goliath to the Israelite army. But even as the Israelite soldiers cried: "Too big! Too big!" there was young David saying: "Yes! Too big to miss!" And so it is with the opportunity to lead someone to Christ – too big to miss. It is normal to feel a few butterflies, but girded with prayer, we can have the amazing privilege of helping precious individuals enter into the most important relationship of their lives, yes, even into eternity.

Some Prerequisites for Evangelism

How do we actually go about it? There are a few prerequisites we should be aware of before getting underway. First and foremost, it is essential that we know Christ ourselves! Like a blind man trying to lecture on color, if we don't have our own relationship with Christ in place, we will have an impossible time trying to lead others to him. We need to have our own testimonies to share and our own experiences of knowing how our Savior Christ has made a difference in our life.

Secondly, we need to have the strong realization that people are lost. Read Luke 15, a three-part single parable on being lost. There Jesus tells us of the lost coin (lost by circumstance), the lost sheep (lost by nature) and the lost son (lost by choice). May Christ give us the urgency for reaching out to those who are lost — yes, by circumstance, nature and choice. Said Jesus: "I have come to seek and to save the lost" (Luke 19:10).

Thirdly, we must love people. May we work to develop a love for the individual, priceless souls God will bring across our paths in a thousand different ways.

Finally, along with a deep recognition that nothing can be done without the Holy Spirit, we must also realize that we do not have to do it all. Those we talk to about Christ may later be led into an actual committed relationship with him by someone else. Likewise, someone else may have previously shared Christ with a person we have the blessing of finally leading to faith in him. The Holy Spirit may allow us to be a link, to share part of the story and to be just part of the process. However, it doesn't hurt to be alert and ready for follow-through later on, should we have the chance again with the same person.

Jesus' Evangelistic Example

Now to practicalities. How do we actually approach someone with the Gospel message? I have found it especially helpful to watch the Master at work when it comes to leading people to him. We are given a wonderful example in John 4, with the story of Jesus and the woman at the well. I have had the privilege of seeing the well at Sychar, and, yes, it is "deep" (vs. 11), and the story here is amazing. It also gives us some key principles in personal evangelism.

1. Be Alert. One might think that all Jesus wanted to do on that hot day was to rest at the side of the well as he waited for his disciples to return from town with food. However, when a lone woman approached to draw water, Jesus was alert and ready to en-

gage her in conversation.

2. Establish contact. Opening the conversation in the most natural way possible, Jesus asked the woman to give him water from the
well. She was thinking about the "water." So that's where he started.
It's important to establish contact on grounds that are comfortable,
by entering into the other person's world and showing interest. Jesus
also allowed the Samaritan woman to minister to him first by drawing water for him. If we are able to be vulnerable to another person, it will often help them to open up and reveal their own points
of need.

3. Arouse curiosity while exposing the need. Jesus, after using
water as the common point of contact, then aroused the Samaritan
woman's curiosity by telling her that he knew of "living water" (vs.
10-16) which would cause her never to be thirsty again. I can just
imagine the woman halting in the midst of drawing water to stare
at this strange man sitting by Jacob's well. "Sir, give me this water .
. ." she said. Jesus had her attention!

4. Address the specific need. Jesus knew, however, that before the
woman could drink of the Living Water, there were areas of hurt,
need and sin in her life that had to be addressed. Because he was
God, he didn't need to be told about her five broken marriages and
current extramarital affair. We, however, will need to take time to
hear individuals' stories and find out what is troubling them. When
Jesus talked with Nicodemus, he uncovered an intellectual need.
For the blind man it was a physical need. Zacchaeus' need had to
do with broken relationships with all the folks he had cheated out
of money.

5. Reveal the heart of the problem. No matter what needs or
hurts or emptiness people may be facing, the heart of the problem
lies in the alienation from God through sin. And this is what we
can help them understand after carefully listening to their stories.
Jesus helps the Samaritan woman to face her own sinful choices by
gently prompting her: "Go, call your husband" (vs. 16). As she con-
fesses that she has no husband and is living with a man, the woman
is forced to face her alienation from God's moral standards.

6. Handle the questions. Like most people, when the truth be-

comes difficult to face, the Samaritan woman next tried to divert the conversation by asking which mountain was the best place for worship, Jerusalem or the Samaritan Mount Gerizim, visible right there near the well. Jesus didn't push aside her question by saying, "No, let's deal with your sin!" He handled her questions, as we must be ready to do, even though they seem to stray from the central topic. The person we are talking with may have serious doubts that need to be honestly and openly discussed. We may not be able to answer everything, but that's okay. Be truthful and try to find someone or some way to get the questions answered. However, do try to discern the real concerns from the false — mere attempts to divert the conversation. The issue could be creation vs. evolution or the existence of God (pretty rare), or the deity of Christ, or the resurrection, or suffering (bad things happening to good people), or even the desperately escapist worries about all the denominations in Christianity or all the hypocrites in the church, or how dull church is! We must respond as best we can to these issues without getting bogged down. Above all, we must impress on people the importance of intellectual honesty and integrity in accepting the conclusion to which all the evidence points. Christianity never suffers from lack of evidence but often suffers from the evidence being ignored.

7. Don't push or force the unready. There are two dangers as people get closer to commitment: forcing the unready or failing to gently push the ready. Feel free to ask people in which category they would put themselves. If they don't feel ready to commit their lives to Christ, try to arrange to see them again at a later point. If that's not possible, handing them a Gospel tract or leaflet is a good idea. Get into the habit of carrying Christian literature with you to give away at times like these.

Don't hesitate to press the ready. When people put themselves in the category of the ready, no matter how timidly they admit it, take the opportunity. Seize the moment! Remember, it's too big to miss! Second Corinthians 6:2 says: "Now is the time of God's favor, now is the day of salvation." Help them to see that delay is actually foolish, since we do not know what tomorrow will bring for us (Proverbs 27:1). I think of the story of the ancient rabbi who was asked by his students: "When shall we repent?"

He replied: "The day before you die."

"But we don't know when we'll die!" they protested.

To which the rabbi shrewdly replied: "Then repent today!"

8. Point them to Jesus and call for a verdict. Probably imagining that she was drawing the conversation to a close, the woman at the well began to procrastinate, delay and postpone by speaking of the day the Messiah would come and give answers to all her questions and problems. She wanted to wait until then. Jesus resisted her inclinations to postpone, as he brought the whole conversation to its most crucial point: "I who speak to you am he" (vs. 26). Faced with Jesus, the Messiah, the Savior of the world, there can be no more evasiveness or avoidance. She is convinced, persuaded.

At this point we lead persons, clearly and decisively, to Jesus Christ, the Savior. Here is the crossroads at which they must decide to repent of sin, believe in Jesus for salvation and choose to follow him only, or turn away. Confront people with the need for a verdict and for decisive action.

After Jesus had revealed that he was indeed the Messiah, the woman at the well's verdict was decisive and her response immediate and total. "Come and see . . ." she said to the people of her town, and "many of the Samaritans from that town believed in him because of the woman's testimony." She made her decision and immediately became a witness, resulting in a great harvest in Sychar that the professional evangelists (the 12 disciples) had totally missed while out buying bread!

This story is a matchless illustration of personal evangelism and witness - a real model for us – Jesus' poor, but privileged, disciples – as we also try to share the Good News with people at a personal level.

Completion and Closure

Now we consider how we bring it all to closure. What must we do? There are, in my view, several things which are key.

1. Summarize. Usually when I have completed the kind of

conversation described here, I try to draw the threads together before moving to closure. I use an A-B-C-D outline, approximately as follows:

A = something to Admit. First of all, people need to be ready to admit their need, whether loneliness, emptiness, boredom, guilt, etc. Whatever the need, the Bible reveals that all human needs ultimately are related to the fact that humans are separated from God by sin. Therefore, people must first admit their need for forgiveness, for a "Forgiver" or Savior.

B = something to Believe. Jesus Christ is the Savior they have just admitted they need and their faith must be focused on and in Christ. One can't just say, "All you need is faith." Faith in what or in whom? Faith has to have a direction and focus if it is to mean anything at all. In Romans 3, Paul says that we are pronounced innocent "through faith in his blood" (vs. 25), i.e., faith in the death of Jesus Christ. People need to put their faith in Jesus Christ and stop believing in good works, church attendance or rituals for salvation. Our faith is in Jesus and his death on the cross – nowhere else.

C = something to Consider. As we come to Christ we have to consider our willingness to leave behind what ruins. Repentance is a turning away from that which ruins, i.e., sinful behavior. If we surrender to Christ as Lord, it implies that we leave behind everything that is a denial of his Lordship. Nor does he necessarily ask us to leave happy, good and worthwhile things. He only asks us to leave what is ruining our lives.

D = something to Do. This now is the moment of truth. People ask: "What must I do?" I usually suggest these three things:

i. Receive Christ as Savior. John 1:12 says: "As many as received him, to them he gave authority to become sons (or children) of God." As one might receive a gift or someone's friendship, we have to receive Christ as our Savior. Faith is the set of hands which reaches out to take Jesus and what he offers: forgiveness, new birth, eternal life and the Holy Spirit as power for living.

ii. Surrender to Christ as Lord. An unconditional surrender, an act of the will, leaves no area of a person's life outside Christ's domain. We now commit our destinies to Jesus Christ. Just as we commit ourselves in faith to a doctor for surgery, a plane for a flight or to another person in marriage, so we must hand ourselves over unreservedly to Jesus in full and willing volitional commitment and trust Jesus Christ as Lord and Master and King.

iii. Finally, we open our hearts to Christ as Friend. Jesus says: "Behold I stand at the door (of your heart) and knock. If anyone hears my voice and opens the door, I will come in." That is his promise. Jesus is true to his promise. If we truly yield to him and truly open to him, he will come in, as he promises to do. A word of testimony from our own experiences of Christ's faithfulness at this point is helpful.

2. Now pray. When people are ready to respond, we now can come to closure and pray something along these lines, sentence by sentence, with them echoing the prayer silently or aloud with us: "Lord Jesus Christ, I admit that I have wandered far away from you. I admit my need for forgiveness. I admit I need a Savior. And I believe that you are the Savior I need. I have also considered the cost of being a Christian and leaving my wayward ways behind. I am serious in this response. I do, therefore, receive you as my Savior. I surrender to you as my Lord and Master and King. And I open my heart to you and ask you to come in. Come in Lord Jesus, by your Holy Spirit, as my Savior, Lord and Friend. I accordingly promise to express my faith in following you and serving you in my home, among my friends, where I work and in your Church. In your name I pray. Amen"

3. Explain the next steps. When people pray this momentous prayer – maybe nervously, with apprehension, or irrepressible fears, or else with cheerfulness and full of abandon, joy and delight, however it happens, we must make sure they grasp some key next steps.

i. Assurance. New disciples needs to receive assurance of salvation based not on feelings but on facts, trusting that the door has truly been opened to Jesus, and he has come in (Rev 3:20).

Also note other scriptures such as Romans 8:38-39 and 1 John 5:11-13, where John talks about how we can "know that (we) have eternal life." This is our birthright and heritage and one of the most glorious spiritual dimensions of the Christian's life. To know – not think, or hope, or guess – that one is a child of God is a blessing beyond compare. Says the old hymn: "Blessed assurance, Jesus is mine/O what a foretaste of glory divine...!" Yes, indeed!

ii. Daily prayer. New disciples must begin to pray and talk to the Lord daily. Prayer is basically talking and communicating with God, and as any friendship requires communication and fellowship to flourish, so it is with our relationship with Christ. We must take time to develop it – even if initially it is only a few minutes each day, and we should plan for this time at the beginning and end of each day. Said one writer: "One of the main reasons so many of God's children don't have a significant prayer life is not so much that we don't want to, but that we don't plan to. If you want renewal in your life of prayer, you must plan to see it."

iii. Daily Bible reading. We must tell new disciples of the importance of reading the scriptures daily and encourage them to start right away – even if only eight or ten verses a day, maybe starting in the Gospels of Mark or John. If they don't have a Bible, help them get one. The New International Version (NIV) is probably the most serviceable and widely used translation at this time, but you could also consider the New Living Bible which is very reader-friendly. As we read the Word of God, we must ask three questions: What does it say? What does it mean? How does it impact me?

iv. Getting into a church. All disciples of Christ have a fundamental necessity of being in a solid church fellowship where the scriptures are faithfully taught, the sacraments dispersed and good teaching offered. Try to steer people to a church fellowship known for its Bible-based teaching and for faithfully proclaiming the Gospel. Inevitably, we will find that many people have been majorly put off by the church. Even so, they belong with the Lord's people and must grasp that an isolated Christian is a contradiction in terms. The church is a self-confessed fellowship of forgiven sinners who acknowledge their inadequacies.

v. Witness. New disciples must begin to witness to others both in word and action. We can't be "secret disciples." The fact is that real discipleship destroys our secrecy, or our secrecy destroys our discipleship. Above all, we need to grasp the truth of Paul Tournier's words: "Our task as lay people is to live our personal communion with Christ with such intensity as to make it contagious."

4. Ongoing contact. If possible, try to establish a means of ongoing contact with your new Christian friends. If they do not live near you, you could keep in touch with them by phone, mail or e-mail. But try not to lose touch.

Now rejoice! After going through this process with a person and coming out the other end with a new brother or sister in Christ, you will discover how fulfilling and exciting this work is! When the disciples in John 4 finally returned from the town with food for Jesus they pressed him to eat. You can just hear the elation in Jesus' voice when he responds to them by saying: "My food is to do the will of him who sent me and to finish his work!" Picture a beaming Savior and some mystified disciples, along with a new believer in the Kingdom and some fresh witness carried out to those in her community!

Gearing the Church for Evangelism

Charles Spurgeon, the great preacher, pastor and evangelist in London, once said to a group of clergy: "Go forward in actual work, for after all we shall be known by what we have done. We ought to be mighty in deed, as well as word. We must have done with daydreams and get to work. Brethren, do something. Do something. Do something. While committees waste their time over resolutions, do something. While societies and unions are making constitutions, let us win souls. Too often we discuss, and discuss and discuss, and Satan laughs up his sleeve. It is time we had done planning and sought something to plan. Our one aim is to save sinners, and this we are not to talk about, but to do in the power of God."

Yes, friends, we can prepare ourselves for evangelism and make great plans for carrying it out, but it is much easier to talk indefinitely about this challenge than to take it up.

Evangelism, I believe, is the primary task of the church. Our Lord's last word in his Great Commission was to go out and preach the Gospel in all the world and make disciples of all nations. And surely his last words must be our first concern.

Indeed, the power of the Holy Spirit, as promised in Acts 1:8, is given so that we may be witnesses in Jerusalem, Judea, Samaria and unto the ends of the earth. If we aren't careful, our congregation can become like an ingrown toenail. You have a group of people who have a lovely, "clubby" time together – the toenail – and the toenail doesn't hurt at first while it is growing in, but after a while it will start to hurt as the "ingrownness" of the group and its exclusive club nature begins to be registered. The spiritual body certainly begins to hurt if it doesn't have a strong outward focus in mission.

Let's think about the local church as a place out of which our evangelism should flow. In many ways, the local church is the best, most logical and most effective vehicle for this activity. It is God's "Plan A." When the church doesn't get on with its task of evangelism, God calls up his "Plan B" and raises up various types of parachurch agencies which will actually go out and do the job in a specific way. But it is the local congregation that should primarily have on its heart the evangelization of its community, region and the world. This cannot be fobbed off on parachurch agencies, useful though they may be. Some people in our churches say: "Oh well, I am not keen on evangelism. I have reservations about certain types of evangelism." So nothing ever happens.

One woman came up to D. L. Moody, the great American evangelist, and said: "Mr. Moody, I don't like the way you do evangelism."

Moody said to her: "Madam, do you do evangelism?"

She replied: "No, I don't."

He countered: "Well, I prefer my way of doing it to your way of not doing it."

We must realize that the Lord's major outreach to the world happens in two primary ways: through the local church and through lay people in the local church. Notice I did not say through the pastors.

Christianity is not primarily an ecclesiastical movement. It is primarily a lay movement. The pastor's task is to train and to activate the workforce of the lay people. Ephesians 4:11-12 says there are different gifts in the Body of Christ "for the equipping of the saints for the work of the ministry." The ministry is not primarily the pastor's job. Ministry is primarily the lay person's job, and a good pastor will ensure that this is the case.

In fact, God is already using mainly lay people to win others to Christ. If I were to ask the members of your church how they came to know the Lord, I can already predict how the majority would answer. The majority of us came to know the Lord through the witness of an individual – not by a radio program, a pastor's sermon or an evangelistic crusade. It's almost foolproof. For example, out of 4,300 international church leaders present at the Lausanne II Congress on World Evangelization in Manila in 1989, more than 3,000 came to know Christ through the witness of another lay person.

So, lay people, God has chosen you to get his message out! Are you doing it? Or are you relying on the pastor to try and do it all for you?

Making a Plan for Evangelism

Once you and your church have grasped that it is up to you to do the job, you have to plan how you are going to do it. This will require establishing your purposes and goals. It is helpful, however, to make a distinction here between a purpose and a goal. A purpose is an arrow which points toward some generally desirable aim. For example, your purpose is to glorify God in your area. But you also need goals. Goals are the stepping stones proceeding ahead in the direction of the arrow to the achievement of that general purpose. The purpose is general and the goals are the stepping stones to achieving your purpose.

Two things characterize a goal: 1) It is accomplishable; 2) It is measurable. For example, if your purpose is to glorify God in your area, one of your goals might involve setting up, through your church, five evangelistic home groups in the next year. This is accomplishable, and it is measurable. At the end of the year, you can see whether you set up five groups, or only two. So many churches have beautiful general purposes, but they have never set goals. Another goal might be to have a local church mission or to establish a missionary prayer group which could begin praying for missionaries or Christian workers locally or abroad. At the end of the year you can easily tell what you have accomplished. And if you didn't accomplish what you had set out to do, you can evaluate what prevented this and thus learn from your mistakes. So I urge you to begin working towards an agreed-upon evangelistic purpose by setting goals for evangelism that are both accomplishable and measurable.

Next, mobilize yourself and others. Decide that you yourself are going to be involved and that you are going to get others involved. A Latin America survey found that the three fastest-growing movements there were the communist party, the Jehovah's Witnesses and the Assemblies of God. Though the messages and beliefs of these three movements are clearly different, the common denominator for the growth they have experienced is that all three movements worked for every-member involvement. When you get a church where every person feels involved in some way, and you are trying to release the gifts in the Body of Christ, things happen. All gifts can be used in the church – graphic design in the church newsletter, electronics for sound systems, teaching, preaching, hospitality, administration, assistance, whatever. But people need a bit of encouragement and they need to be mobilized and trained. This is the pastor's job.

Keeping Your Evangelism Strategic
In order to keep your church's evangelistic vision strategic and ap-

propriate, I want to suggest to you a formula called "R–A–C" that is used by some of the rapidly growing churches in Latin America. In this formula: R = Reflection; A = Action; and C = Consolidation.

1. Reflection. As a church, you need to stop and think about your evangelistic program. As one observer said: "There are two great dangers in evangelism. One is to change the message and the other is to refuse to change the method!" We must be willing to evaluate our methods and write over the door of our church the word "THINK" in letters of fire. Many churches are terrified of evaluation.

We have to stop and ask ourselves: "Are the structures of our church helping or hindering the process of evangelization and outreach? Is the church leadership helping or hindering, blocking or releasing? Are lay people willing to be trained in evangelism? If not, why not? Are our services "user-friendly" to inquirers or new converts? And are we using all the gifts in our fellowship, especially the evangelistic ones?"

In evaluation, we will also seek to be "loving critics" who produce creative change, rather than "uncritical lovers" who block and stifle, or "unloving critics" who destroy, wound and hurt. Evaluation thus requires loving critics, not uncritical lovers or unloving critics.

2. Action. When we come to putting things into action, there are several key steps in the process. The first is that we have to win the victory in prayer. Whatever we are talking about doing, prayer will be where it is born and where we will get clarity about what to do. Prayer is where the Lord gives us the victory ahead of time. We can't go out into these assignments without a strong working base of prayer.

Secondly, we have to cultivate the evangelistic vision and then find people who will respond to the vision. If a pastor helps his people reach an exciting vision of what can be done in the town or community, people will indeed get excited about it. They will want to move on it. Maybe pray the Jabez prayer: "Lord, enlarge our territories" (1 Chronicles 4:10). In this process, people also have to be challenged to put their pocketbooks on the line. If fresh outreach from the church is to be motivated, it may require some further finances. So challenging people in terms of their giving and stewardship for mission and evangelism is key. People enjoy giving to a significant missionary vision, and mission-minded, evangelistic churches seldom have financial struggles.

Ultimately, after planning, prayer and new financial giving, we have to get our church members acting together to accomplish evangelism within the community. I had a friend in San José, Costa Rica, who once wrote an article entitled "The Church Building – Means or End?" In it, he asked if the church building is the end of the line, or if it is a means to something out there in the world. My friend had a church in San José where his people came to church, had a time of worship, prayer, teaching, inspiration and training, and then the whole church would disperse into the streets of the city. Then the church would reconvene an hour later with all the members bringing back the people they had brought to Christ or contacted while out witnessing in the streets! That sort of thing shatters normal stereotypes, but why not? Other options could be: planning a local church mission; mounting a visiting evangelistic campaign; teaching personal evangelism; initiating new discipleship courses; establishing a regular guest service; organizing some evangelistic symposia; putting on an evangelistic youth concert or film series; equipping home group leaders to be effective evangelists; and so on.

3. Consolidation. When the evangelism has been implemented, peg down the new ground that has been captured and consolidate it. That is, make sure new believers and new members are being discipled, are in fellowship groups and are becoming part of the church. Then reflect again, act again and consolidate again. Reflection – Action – Consolidation: R–A–C, over and over again.

Gearing the local church for evangelism means gearing and equipping ourselves, witnessing, evaluating and using our homes. It could mean having a special mission or calling in a parachurch agency. It could mean using a visiting campaign or a monthly guest service. If you know your pastor will be doing an evangelistic sermon, say, the third Sunday of every month, geared for the outsider or non-Christian, you can plan ahead to bring an uncommitted friend. These are all things for your consideration and experimentation. Why not take just one idea and try to get it going in your church? You've got nothing to lose and a vibrant, growing church to gain!

Developing our personal testimony, learning to lead people to Christ and participating in a local congregation in action to reach the lost is the charge and privilege of every believer. I hope through this book, you came to realize that you don't necessarily have to be highly educated, well-off or even well-connected to be a missionary. Faith in God and willingness is all that's really needed. When you look at it that way, you can also be a missionary, can't you?

Narciso Zamora walks the message of Christ into the mountains, jungles, fields and forests of his native Peru and throughout Ecuador and Chile. Dreading the life of hard labor offset by nights of drunken stupor that his father modeled, Zamora ran away from home after high school. He lived a vagrant's life, surviving through delinquency, until through the generous support of a Christian family, Zamora came to know Christ. He left the jungle to study at a seminary in Lima.

Walking Man recounts Zamora's winding and treacherous path, literally and figuratively, toward finding his calling in missions. Characteristic of Zamora's more than 30 years of mission experiences is his determination to go anywhere he felt called to preach and teach – walking day and night into the jungle or trekking from valley to alpine zone and back down the other side of the mountain, just to reach an isolated village.

With half a dozen well-established congregations in place in Peru, Zamora affiliated the churches with an international denomination and later moved to Ecuador and Chile planting churches.

In Chile, a new trial faced the Zamora family when his wife's kidneys started to fail. Dealing with the emotional turmoil of a chronically ill spouse wore more heavily on him than any adversity he had encountered in his ministry. Zamora became depressed and in this chapter of his life, he learned new lessons and gained new insights about what it means to carry the cross of Christ.

Walking Man is a cross-cultural reading experience that tells a compelling story that and generates due interest in Latin American missions. For more, visit www.walkingman.ws.

Michael Cassidy is the founder of African Enterprise, a ministry of evangelism, leadership development, reconciliation, and aid, which he launched in 1961 with the ultimate aim of evangelizing the cities of Africa through word and deed in partnership with the Church.

Cassidy was born in Johannesburg, South Africa, and became a Christian as a student at Cambridge University in England, and received a call from God to city evangelism in Africa while participating in the 1957 Billy Graham Crusade in New York. African Enterprise encompasses teams in Congo (DRC), Ethiopia, Ghana, Kenya, Malawi, Rwanda, Tanzania, Uganda and Zimbabwe and South Africa. Cassidy and his wife, Carol, live in Pietermaritzburg and have three married children and five grandchildren. For more information, please contact: African Enterprise, PO Box 727 • Monrovia, CA 91017 • 626.357.8811 • www.africanenterprise.org.

Continue Your Journey with Walking Man

If you enjoyed this book, why not give a copy to a friend, your local library, church library or a social services organization that helps people who need inspiration? Take advantage of this easy order form and **pay no shipping fees or taxes** on your purchase!

Please send me at $12.95 for each copy or $10 per copy for 10 or more copies of any combination of versions:

_____ copies of *Walking Man* in print in English

_____ copies of *Walking Man* on CD (audiobook)

_____ copies of *Walking Man* in print in Spanish (*Caminante con Dios*)

_____ copies of *Walking Man* in Spanish (*Caminante con Dios*) on CD (audiobook)

Walking Man is also available for purchase in all of the above formats and in e-book ($4.95) in English at www.walkingman.ws. Download the Spanish e-book version for free!

Mail this form with check, money order or credit card information to:
        The Quilldriver
        PO Box 573
        Clarksville, AR 72830   Or fax to: 479-497-0321

Name_____
Address_____
_____
City_____State_____Zip_____
Credit Card (Visa/MC) #_____
Expiration Date__/__ Name on Card_____
E-mail for purchase confirmation_____

Easy Calculator
2 x $12.95 = $25.90   6 x $12.95 = $77.70
3 x $12.95 = $38.85   7 x $12.95 = $90.65
4 x $12.95 = $51.80   8 x $12.95 = $103. 60
5 x $12.95 = $64.75   For 10 or more copies, all copies are $10 each.